The Aswang Complex
in Philippine Folklore

MAXIMO D. RAMOS

PHOENIX PUBLISHING HOUSE
927 Quezon Avenue, Quezon City

Contents

VISCERA SUCKER LEGENDS

WITCH LEGENDS

LEGENDS ABOUT ASWANG
OF UNDETERMINED CATEGORY

Foreword

THE PUBLICATION OF THIS BOOK is a bold attempt to present to the reader and to students of Filipino society and culture one of the dominant Filipino beliefs, the aswang. For some strange reason the belief has never been explored for its usefulness in the field of literature or social studies. Even educators shy away from it, branding the belief as superstitious and therefore not to be perpetuated. While this view is entertained, however, there is continued use in the schools—including the nursery schools—of Western tales like "Hansel and Gretel," "Rapunzel," "Snow White," and so forth, dealing with witches, dwarfs, and other people of lower mythology. It is sad to note that while we accept these stories as entertaining to our children, we reject our own folktales about equivalent characters as superstitious and undesirable.

It is about time that we changed our perspective, that we accepted our own literary heritage and used it if we are to make education meaningful to our children. Maximo D. Ramos has provided us with one way to achieve this. Of course the present volume is only one of his many works on Philippine folklore.

While he presents the materials in this book as folklore, these can also be regarded as ethnographic data in that they deal with one of the dominant aspects of

Filipino folk culture. The aswang belief may be viewed as socially functional in many communities. Our own field notes on the subject matter indicate that aswang tales are used by many people as a medium of social control. For example, when a child frets at night or becomes unruly during the day, adult members of the family or sibling caretakers generally use the aswang belief as a means of quieting the child or of disciplining him. When one wishes to protect his fields from unnecessary trespass by others, all he has to do is make it known that an aswang haunts the place and no one will dare enter the premises, especially at night. Deviant behavior is also handled through avoidance, and the aswang label is handy for this purpose. Once the label is set, deviants are either coerced into conformity to what is acceptable behavior or are effectively deprived of their legitimate status in the community.

Thus seen, it is understandable that the aswang belief has persisted in our society over such a long period of time. The earliest reference to the belief is in Miguel de Loarca's account of the customs and practices of the Pintados of Panay in 1582-83, and the first mention of its existence among the Tagalogs is in Juan de Plasencia's account in 1588-91. Other chroniclers who wrote about the Philippines thereafter also mentioned the aswang as one aspect of the native belief system. In 1949, Fr. Frank Lynch wrote the first analytical study of the aswang belief among the Bicolanos. But the present book by Maximo D. Ramos is the most comprehensive collection of aswang stories ever put together. This is indeed a welcome volume.

Ramos divides his narrative data into six categories: the *vampire stories*, in which the aswang appear as blood-sucking creatures, generally in the form of beautiful women; the *viscera sucker accounts*, where the aswang are characterized as buxum, long-haired, and light-complexioned females who are fond of human innards; the *weredog accounts*, where the aswang are seen as powerful beings who transform themselves into dogs (or other beasts) before they attack their victims; the *witch tales*, in which the aswang are recognized as mean, vindictive old women; the *ghoul stories*, where the aswang are described as beings who are fond of human flesh, particularly those of dead persons; and the tales in which the traits and activities of aswang do not make it possible to place them under the said headings—a situation, as Dr. Ramos explains in the book, characteristic of many folk beliefs.

In presenting these stories, Ramos skillfully takes us into another world of experience which is so alien to ours — an experience characterized by non-ordinary reality but exceedingly real to those who participate in the encounters. The central importance of this contrast in experiences lies in the fact that our world is real only as our culture allows us to experience it. The accounts of aswang encounters included in this book reveal another realm of experience which many of us cannot understand because our world is presented to us in a different construct. But by entering into this other world of the rural folk through the accounts narrated here, we can see better our own world and are thereby enabled to appreciate that of others, to realize that the difference between the two worlds of experience is a matter of cultural orientation.

And herein lies the lasting contribution of Maximo D. Ramos not only to the study of Philippine folklore in particular but also to the understanding of Filipino society and culture in general. This book is a must for those who seek to explore the fascinating world of Filipino supernatural experience.

F. LANDA JOCANO
Former Chairman
Department of Anthropology
University of the Philippines

From The Publisher

MAXIMO D. RAMOS, the first editor in chief of Phoenix Publishing House, was associated with the company from 1963 until his death on December 12, 1988. As editor and consultant, he gathered together a team of teachers who were creative, understood the needs of Filipino students, knew their pedagogy, and, above all, were committed to the ideals of nationhood espoused by my father, Dr. Ernesto Y. Sibal.

The present leadership of Phoenix Publishing House in the textbook field in all subject areas on all three levels of the educational system is due, in a large measure, to the unfaltering loyalty and passion for work of Dr. Ramos.

Dr. Ramos never relaxed his own personal pursuit of the Muse and continued to write short stories, poems, and essays. At the same time, he devoted special attention to serious research on Philippine mythology and folklore. All these were done as he taught and performed administrative duties at the Philippine Normal College and later at the University of the East.

Phoenix Publishing House takes pride in publishing these ten volumes of the essential works of Dr. Ramos. We know that his legacy will fire the imagination of Filipino students and inspire them to know more about their own folkways and folklore and to write them down for others to enjoy and appreciate. Dr. Ramos's only limitation perhaps is access to Filipino language as medium of his literary output. But he has shown the Filipino student that one can master the English language and use it to advantage in portraying Philippine reality. And because the setting is Filipino and the experiences are part of the Filipino tradition, we know that his writings will appeal to children and to adults as well.

His works, collectively titled REALMS OF MYTHS AND REALITY, consist of the following:

This collection is our tribute to Dr. Maximo D. Ramos and our contribution to Filipiniana.

J. ERNESTO SIBAL
Publisher

The Aswang Complex in Philippine Folklore[*]

"WHAT'S AN ASWANG?" once asked Wayland D. Hand,[1] fascinated by the conflicting traits glimpsed through the scattered material about this mythical being. I rashly volunteered to find out, little knowing that the search was to get me into unexplored territory and that to answer Dr. Hand's question I must first categorize and classify the traits and functions of just about the entire lower Philippine pantheon.[2]

This paper is a report on my findings about the aswang. But I must caution the reader that because of the distance and the cultural variables involved, the creatures of lower mythology[3] in this part of the globe do not fit exactly into the traditional European catego-

---

[*] Paper read at the meeting of the Philippine Folkore Society, January 21, 1968. A shorter version of this paper appeared in *Western Folklore*, XXVIII (October, 1969), 238-49.

[1] Former president of the American Folklore Society, former editor of the *Journal of American Folkore* and of *Western Folklore*, and Director of the Center for the Study of Comparative Folklore and Mythology, University of California, Los Angeles, where he teaches a course on the creatures of lower mythology.

[2] Maximo Ramos, "A Study of Lower Creatures in Philippine Mythology, With Implications for Education' (Ph.D. dissertation, University of the Philippine, Quezon City, 1965; published by the University of the Philippines Press, 1965).

[3] "The creatures of lower mythology are fabular beings below the rank of ghosts, ancestral spirits, saints, angels, and beneficent deities." Wayland D.

ries, although, as Thompson well observed concerning mythical creatures in various areas of the world:

> Many of them are doubtless related to those of neighboring lands, but exact equations of similar creatures [are] usually dangerous, or at least inaccurate...

> In spite of these striking regional differences there are no definite cultural boundaries, and many of the concepts relating to supernatural creatures are found with little change over whole continents, and sometimes, indeed over the whole earth.[4]

It would be helpful for purposes of comparative study to recognize convergences where these exist.

The aswang concept is most usefully understood as a congeries of beliefs about five types of mythical beings identifiable with certain creatures of the European tradition: (1) the blood-sucking vampire, (2) the self-segmenting viscera sucker, (3) the man-eating weredog, (4) the vindictive or evil-eye witch, and (5) the carrion-eating ghoul. Thus when Philippine folk speak of the aswang, they generally refer to the physical traits, habitat, or activities of these five types of mythical beings, and sometimes also of other mythical entities like the demon, dwarf, and elf. This transfer of traits and functions is characteristic of oral traditions, and it is the business of the student to clear up the confusion. By relating, if he can, the physical traits and functions of each creature with those of the lower mythical beings of European folklore, he can help future students do further research on the subject in relation to studies in that better ordered tradition. Unless this is first done, the student can

---

Hand, lectures on creatures of lower mythology, University of California, Los Angeles, Feb. 7, 1963. Generally maleficent, the creatures of lower mythology have grown even more so as a result of contacts with later faiths whose agents must not only scorn but denigrate the gods which it is their mission to banish. In his summary of the pre-Indic and pre-Islamic cultures of Southeast Asia, Cole wrote: "Religious practices centered around a host of spirits, some good, some bad, which had to be propitiated" (Fay-Cooper Cole, *The Peoples of Malaysia* [Princeton, 1946], p. 243).

[4] Stith Thompson, *The Folktale* (New York, 1946), p. 243.

be lost in the formidable tangle of beliefs about the lower mythical beings known by a wide variety of local names in an archipelago like the Philippines' seven thousand islands and some eighty-five native languages—languages, not just dialects, since the speakers of one tongue cannot communicate with those of any other—represented by the vernacular texts in part II of this book.

What follows is a brief description of each aspect of the aswang, a term chiefly used by the Tagalog, Bikol, and Visayan groups in the country.[5] Some cultural patterns that evolved from the beliefs concerning each aspect will also be mentioned.

THE VAMPIRE

By Philippine folk traditions, the vampire is a blood-sucking creature disguised as a beautiful maiden. It marries an unsuspecting youth and thus can sip a little of his blood each night till he dies of anemia, whereupon the monster gets itself another husband. To suck blood the vampire uses the tip of its tongue, pointed like the proboscis of a mosquito, to pierce the jugular vein.

In some cases the vampire leaves its spouse unharmed and only uses his home as an operations base. It flies out at night to raid other villages. Like human malefactors, it does not ply its trade in the vicinity of its domicile for fear of exposing its true nature.

Some Philipine vampires die but come back, like the revenants of European folklore, to suck blood. They sleep all day in deep woods far from human communities, unlike the vampires of the Slavic belt, which are said to remain in the tomb and there lie asleep except when they emerge once a week to quench their thirst for fresh human blood.

---

[5] Here, however, some caution is necessary: "But the reader is warned again that the placing of beliefs and practices on paper gives them a coherence and acceptance far beyond that in the mind of any one individual or group of individuals" (Cole, *op. cit.*, p. 76).

Other Philippine names for the blood-sucking aswang are *amalanhig* ('the stiff one') among the West Visayans, *danag* among the Isneg, and *mandurugo* ('the blood-sucker') among the Tagalog.

The beliefs current among Filipino folk concerning vampires are in part responsible for the endogamous tendencies of Philippine groups. Parents prefer to marry off their offspring into families that they have known rather well because in early times there was fear that a handsome stranger might be a vampire. This fear, added to the desire of mestizos to marry among themselves for reasons of race and from a wish to keep the family property intact, has blocked the enculturation of Filipinos of white extraction in the provincial towns. These beliefs have also lent support to the divisive tendencies among Philippine groups, since folk from other villages might often be suspect of being vampires.

THE VISCERA SUCKER

The viscera sucker is a mythical being said to suck out the internal organs (*naguneg* in Iloko, *laman luob* in Tagalog, *kasudlan* in West Visayan) or to feed on the voided phlegm of the sick.[6] This creature rarely occurs in European folklore but is widespread in Malaysia. It is reported to look like an attractive woman by day, buxom, long-haired, and light-complexioned. Its tongue is extended, narrow, and tubular like a dinking straw — but not pointed like the vampire's— and it is capable of being distended to a great length. At night the monster discards its lower body from the waist down and flies or floats or glides out.[7]

---

[6] In Cambodia the viscera sucker is called *srei ap* and is said to feed on human excreta. The *srei ap* are described as folows: "At night their heads, accompanied only by the alimentary canal, wander about to feed on excrements, in search of which they will even look among the intestines of people who are asleep" (*Encylopedia of Religion and Ethics* [Edinburgh, 1908], III, 158).

[7] From this habit derives its Tagalog name of *manananggal* (fr. Malay *tanggal*, 'to detach', plus a particle meaning 'one who is in the habit of or is

The creature conceals its discarded member beneath the bedsheet, inside a closet, or in the backyard. A banana grove in the yard is especialy suited for this purpose since banana trunks resemble human legs. The creature then gets to the roof of the house it has marked out for attack. It looks for a hole in the thatch and, finding one, inserts its tongue, elongating it and making it as fine as thread so that it can hardly be detected while it swings about till it touches down and enters the body of a sleeper and then seeks out his heart, liver, lungs, spleen, and entrails.[8]

An expectant mother is a choice victim of the viscera sucker, its objective being to suck its baby dry, killing it. A viscera sucker may also cling to the floor joist under the bed of a tubercular or asthmatic person and suck his voided phlegm. Viscera suckers, it is said, are stopped because of their habit of prowling under houses.

Should the creature's discarded body be moved even slightly or the cut portion be sprinkled over with ashes, vinegar, spices, or salt, the viscera sucker cannot be whole again and dies unless it can persuade a human being to return the body where it was before or wash off these substances with water before dawn.

Some viscera suckers are said to live in the jungle by day. They throw their arms over a branch, drape their hair over their faces, and sleep all day.[9] Other viscera

---

expert at.'). The Indonesian viscera sucker is said to cast off its entire body from the neck down and, with its hair as a propellant, its head and entrails fly out at night to seek human viscera (*Encylopedia of Religion and Ethics*, VII, 237). Informants from Leyte and Capiz said that the viscera sucker bends from the waist for about five minutes until her lower body detaches itself. An informant from Catanduanes Island said that the viscera sucker stares at the full moon until gooey tears fall from its eyes and then its upper body glides out. An informant from Albay added that the viscera sucker has holes in its armpits to drop oil into before it flies out. Informants from Atimonan, Quezon, reported that the viscera sucker discards its lower extremities from the knees down before flying out to forage.

[8] Asked how these large organs can pass through such a narrow conduit, an informant from Central Luzon replied that the creature uses its sharp nails to incise the body of its victim and then reaches in with its hand instead.

[9] Vampires, viscera suckers, and a number of other Philippine lower mythological beings are said to be particularly active between twelve

suckers dwell in lonely huts deep in the woods, but like vampires most of them reside in human communities with the men they have married.

Viscera suckers fear knives, light, salt, spices, ashes, large crustanceans, and the sting ray's tail. It is said that the most effective way to kill a viscera sucker is to thrust the sharpened top end of a bamboo into its back.

Other names by which the viscera sucking aswang is known in various sections of the country are *abat* among the East Visayan, *aswang na lupad* ('flying aswang') among the Bikol, *boruka* (a corrupted form of the Spanish *bruja*, 'witch') among the Iloko, *manananggal* among the Tagalog, and *mangalok* among the Cuyonon.

Beliefs concerning the viscera sucker may have helped set the custom, still common in Philippine rural communities, of sleeping prone. This position, is said to hide the sleeper's bodily orifices from the viscera sucker's probing tongue. In many Philippine villages, too, houses have their windows on two opposite sides only; the household members sleep in alternate positions to afford, it is said, optimum vigilance against viscera suckers since there is an even distribution of eyes directed at either side of the house.

The extended family setup in the Philippines and the rapid pace of the country's population growth, which according to United Nations figures is among the two or three fastest in the world, have in part resulted from the feeling that small families are vulnerable to viscera sucker attack. The home in many rural Philippine villages is typically a one-room affair; cooking, eating, working, sitting, and sleeping are all done in that single room. Family members sleep together on a single mat on the floor under a large mosquito net.[10]

---

midnight and about three in the morning. This belief may be an accretion from the European Middle Ages, since the period coincides with the "witching hour" there, the three-hour gap in the dead of night between Matins or the midnight mass and Lauds at three, both marked by the tolling of the church bells. See Genevieve d'Haucourt, *Life in the Middle Ages*, trans. Veronica Hull and Christopher Fernau (New York, 1963), p. 50.

[10] The story is told of an American Fulbright researcher whose host

The ready acceptance of purpueral confinements in modern hospitals can in part be credited to the relative security of tin roofs and concrete buildings against viscera suckers. Writers have long attributed the steep pitch of the old-type Philippine thatched roof to the heavy tropical rainfall even in relatively arid regions of the country. In view of the beliefs concerning the aswang, I suggest that steep roofs became fashionable because of the notion that the viscera sucker, vampire, ghoul, and witch would have a harder time balancing themselves on such a roof than on a flat one. This inference gains support from the frequent use of crossed bamboo staves, sharpened at the upper ends, to weigh down the rooftree—an architectural detail that may have developed after Christianization, for it does not appear in old prints of indigenous Philippine houses. One of the most effective countermeasures against all types of aswang, it will be recalled, is sharpened bamboo.

Again, the gables of many a Philippine roof feature an ornamental sharp cone of tin. Though the artistic effect of the ornament is undoubted, there is a possibility that its reputed virtue in keeping the aswang creatures off the roof may have been a strong reason for its widespread use in the country. Another feature of many Philippine homes, especially among the more affluent in Mindanao, is the use of elaborately carved beam-ends showing highly stylized fierce-looking crocodiles and pythons. My notes indicate that the ancient Filipinos regarded crocodiles and pythons as dragons and worshipped them. These types of house decor may therefore have started as a protection against the aswang, too. Beliefs in viscera suckers also help explain why many Filipinos refuse to sleep at the center of a room, preferring the sides instead.[11]

---

begged him to sleep with his entire family, including unmarried maidens, instead of elsewhere on the floor. He was told that the family liked him too much to consign him to a separate bed. He could not understand why until he learned about the viscera sucker's method of attack.

[11] But not too close to a post, for the posts may harbor a tree-dwelling

In San Narciso, Zambales, where immigrants from Paoay, Ilocos Norte, settled early in the nineteenth century and probably brought over their Iloko folk beliefs, children are discouraged from sleeping at the center of the room (and between their parents) by the belief that about midnight a harmful mythical being, perhaps a viscera sucker, entered the house and said:

> Diak kayat ti nakinigid,
> Agallugit;
> Kayatko ti nagtingnga,
> Agammantika.

> (I don't want the one at the edge,
> He smells like chicken droppings;
> I want the one in the middle,
> He smells like pork lard.)

Upon hearing about this belief, Aurora P. Olaguer, a zoology professor from Guinobatan, Albay, said in an interview on June 15, 1970, that an equivalent mythical being was believed by Bikol folk to say on entering a house late at night:

> Sa butnga sakluton,
> Sa gilid kibliton.

> (I'll snatch [with claws] the one in the middle,
> I'll tickle [with fingers] the one at the sides.)

Beliefs concerning vampires and viscera suckers help explain why rural Filipinos hang at the eaves of their homes the carapaces of marine crabs, lobsters, prawns, and stuffed sea fish, especially the more ferocious look-

---

mythical demon like the bangungot or batibat. This is a nightmare-inducing, insanity-causing creature resembling the genii of the Near East. It is said to have refused to leave its tree when it was felled and stubbornly to have gone on living in a crevice or cavity in the wood, emerging to sit on a tenant's chest and suffocate him by plugging his mouth with its phallus and his nostrils with its testicles.

ing species, such as the globefish. The aswang is said to fear salt, and marine fish serve to remind it of their salt-water habitat.[12]

These beliefs, finally, also suggest an explanation for the Filipino's fondness for salt, sour, and spicy foods since, as stated earlier, these are considered effective repellents against the aswang, and the cooking and eating of food with a strong dash of these indredients would serve, it is thought, to ward off these maleficent beings.

THE WEREDOG

The weredog is a mythical being said to be a man or woman— chiefly the former—by day, but at night to turn into a ferocious beast, principally a dog, known as *aso* in many Philippine languages.[13] A werefolf [14] is identified with the fiercest animal in a region, so that Europe has werewolves, China werefoxes, and India weretigers. Since there are no wolves in the Philippines, the term *weredog* is more appropriate; although the term *werebeast* may, in some cases, be even more applicable.

A weredog is said to reside in a village and turn into a ferocious dog, boar, or large cat at about midnight.[15]

---

[12] In Europe, "evil spirits," more strictly identifiable as lower mythological beings as construed here, are said to avoid bodies of water, e.g. witches cannot cross a river or sea.

[13] The word *aswang* itself is perhaps a telescope form of *asu-asuan* ('the likeness of a dog').

[14] "Literally, the term *werewolf* (from O.E. *wer*, man, plus *wulf*, wolf): a human being transformed into a wolf by bewitchment, or one having the power to assume wolf-form at will" (Maria Leach, ed., *Funk and Wagnalls, Standard Dictionary of Folklore, Mythology and Legend* [New York, 1949-50], II, p. 1170).

[15] The Philippine demons are said to do so, too, another case of trait and functions transfer. In "A Study of Lower Creatures in Philippine Mythology," I have identified and described twelve types of harmful fabular creatures.

xxiii

Then it attacks villagers, even entering homes and setting upon youngsters who cry too much.[16] It sinks its fangs into the victim's neck and bites or even devours him. It attacks pregnant women who are on the road at night and who neglect to let their long hair hang loose.

Both the weredog and the viscera sucker are said to acquire their taste for human flesh by having eaten food which another weredog or viscera sucker spat on or licked with its tongue. It is also said to acquire this peculiar taste after voluntarily swallowing a creature resembling a black chick which pops out of the mouth of a dying old weredog or viscera sucker. The chick dwells in the creature's stomach and shares the food its host eats.[17]

Weredogs dread the same things which vampires, viscera suckers, and witches fear. But weredogs and witches are especially afraid of the sting ray's tail. The popularity of ray's tail as an appurtenance among rural wayfarers is born of widespread fears of the aswang. The weredog can get away after a switching with a ray's tail, but its wounds are said to appear on the body of the man it turns into the next day.

The weredog aspect of the aswang is also known as *kiwig* ('sloping') in Aklanon, *malakat* ('walker') in Cebu Visayan, and aswang *na lakaw* ('walking aswang') in Bikol.

In some parts of the country there is considerable hostility to peddlers, especially those known to come from provinces reputed as the home of aswang, such as Sorsogon and Tabaco, Albay, in the Bicol region and

---

[16] The utility of such a belief in making children fall into line is obvious.
[17] For these reasons, many rural folk consider the weredog and viscera sucker state as an affliction deserving of sympathy. A youth who finds that the pretty girl (or vice versa) he plans to marry, or has married, is a viscera sucker or weredog can help her disgorge the chick by either of two standard procedures: (1) making her sit on a swing suspended from a high branch, winding the rope, then letting the rope undo itself, thus dizzying her, and repeating the process till she retches and expels the parasite from her stomach; or (2) lashing her upside down to a tree and smudging her till the smoke makes her regurgitate the parasite.

Aklan and Capiz in the Western Visayas. The folk fear that weredogs take the guise of peddlers in order to enter communities, and they say they linger in neighborhoods where expectant mothers reside.[18] Laborers on government construction jobs are often under a heavy cloud of suspicion in the villages, and particularly so if they are known to come from the areas just named. Food is freely exchanged among neighbors, but where the aswang belief persists, Filipinos seldom accept gifts of food from strangers.

In the past, cascading long hair was idealized among Filipino women, especially those who were pregnant. This was because it was thought that long hair protected expectant mothers against weredogs.

THE WITCHES

Another member of the cluster of mythical concepts encompassed by the term *aswang* is the witch, believed by the folk to be a man or woman—mostly the latter—who is extremely vindictive or who causes sickness without meaning to do so. By magically intruding various objects—shells, bone, unhusked rice, fish, and insects of various species—through the victim's bodily orifices or by herself entering the victim's body, the Philippine witch punishes those by whom she has been put out. Or by an innocent look or remark, she also makes an equally innocent victim ill. Unlike the European witches, however, the Philippine witch has no appetite for human flesh. She is shy and lives in abandoned houses at the outskirts of towns and villages. She will not look people straight in the eye because the image in the pupils of her eyes is said to be upside down and the pupils are thin and elongated like a cat's or lizard's in bright sunshine.

---

[18] An informant from Marikina, Rizal, reported that a weredog would sit sniffing around at a street crossing by night. To a weredog a fetus in the mother's womb smells as sweet as *pinipig*, or young glutinous rice roasted and hulled in a mortar.

The list of objects useful in fighting witches is long, and this is fortunate because the fear of these creatures is widespread in the archipelago, a fear keyed even higher by the beliefs brought into the country by the Spaniards during their conquest and colonization of the archipelago in the sixteenth and seventeenth centuries when, it will be recalled, witch hunts gripped Europe. These countermeasures have been classified as certain plants, the smoke of certain burning objects, certain objects found in the home, certain practices, and certain sea fish, particularly, as mentioned earlier, the tail of the sting ray.[19]

Other names by which the witch aspect of the aswang is known in the Philippines are *mambabarang* among the Bikol, *manggagamod* among the Iloko and Pangasinan, *mamumuyag* among the West Visayan, and *mangkukulam* among the Pampango and Tagalog.

The beliefs concerning witches help explain why a sting ray's tail can often be found hidden behind the thatched door in rural Philippine homes. It is commonly believed that if a witch has entered the body of someone in the family, it can be evicted by thrashing the patient with the ray's tail until the witch abandons its host. The Filipino parent's readiness to thrash his recalcitrant offspring with the ray's tail or a rattan whip is not just his quickness to apply a disciplinary measure but as arising from his eagerness to exorcise any witch that may have entered the youngster's body, thereby making him ornery.

Since insects are in many areas thought to be agents of witches, Filipinos are wary of these in their homes, especially at night. The Filipino's lack of affection for pet dogs and their aversion to little creatures generally may be a function of their forebears' fear that these were agents of the aswang.[20]

---

[19] Francis X. Lynch, "An Mga Asuwang: A Bikol Belief," *Philippine Social Sciences and Humanities Review*, XIV (Dec. 1949), 416-17.

[20] But the Filipino is relatively fond of the cat, which in the Philippines is rarely considered a familiar of the witch and in at least one folktale protects its human mistress against an ogre.

Filipinos have an evasive glance; they are not as a rule in the habit of looking one another straight in the eye. This is a behavior pattern they may have inherited from forebears who feared that one who looked at another directly in the eye could be suspected as nosing about for witches. Because of the Filipinos' evasive glance, Westerners often mistake them for being bashful when they are merely being prudent.

The belief in witches has helped develop an extremely polite people, for it is said that one who treats a witch crossly will be swiftly taken ill.

THE GHOUL

The Philippine ghoul is said to steal human corpses and devour them. For this purpose, its nails are horny, curved, and sharp and its teeth pointed. Its smell and breath are fetid, and though generally invisible, the creature is said to look like a human being when it shows itself.

Some ghouls live in human communities. At night they congregate in large trees near a cemetery and then descend and exhume the newly buried corpses. They devour their plunder, making audible noises as they do so. A ghoul is said to be able to hear, over great distances, the groans of the dying. Its greed is aroused when it catches the scent of death, and then it snatches the mourners as well as the dead.[21]

---

[21] Cf. Malinowski's description of the *mulukuausi*, the dreaded ghosts believed in by the Trobriand Islanders, who share a good number of folk beliefs with the Filipinos to the northwest: " . . . they [*mulukuausi*] are possessed of truly ghoulish instincts. Whenever a man dies, they simply swarm and feed on his insides. They eat away his *lopoula* [translated 'lungs', also denotes the "insides" in general.—M.'s note. There seems to be a transfer of food preferences here. As noted above, the internal organs are the favorite food of the viscera sucker.—R.], his tongue, his eyes, and, in fact, all his body, after which they become even more than ever dangerous to the living. They assemble all round the house where the dead man lived and try to enter it. In the old days, when the corpse was exposed in the middle of the village in a half-covered grave, the *mulukuausi* used to congregate on the trees in and around the village. When the body is carried into the grave to be buried, magic is used to ward off the *mulukuausi*.

According to Philippine traditional beliefs, the ghoul can be frightened off by fire, loud noises, metals, and spicy foods. Even Lumawig, the chief deity of Bontok higher mythology, showed irritation at the presence of a red pepper bush near the house in the Earth World where he came to live after marrying an Earth maiden. During the mortuary vigil the early Filipinos had a bonfire blazing beside the dead in order to keep the ghouls at a safe distance. Fear of the trees growing beside cemeteries is general among Filipinos.[22]

Filipino village folk leave sharp bladed weapons dangling between the slats in the bamboo floor at night to make the ghouls stay away. They wash the corpse with vinegar and strong-smelling simples to ward off ghouls, for these monsters are said to congregate invisibly on the bier or coffin and replace it with a banana trunk that they have first made to look exactly like the deceased, although the more knowledgeable among the people will discover that the substitute leaves no fingerprints. Then, spiriting the corpse off after first turning it

---

"The *mulukuausi* are intimately connected with the smell of carrion...

"The *mulukuausi* are objects of real terror. Thus the immediate neighborhood of the grave is absolutely deserted when night approaches...

"Even in and around the village where a death has occurred there is the greatest fear of the *mulukuausi*, and at night the natives [who Malinowski notes do not otherwise fear the dark.—R.] refuse to go about the village or to enter the surrounding grove and gardens. I have often questioned natives as to the real danger of walking about alone at night soon after a man died, and there was never the slightest doubt that the only beings to be dreaded were the *mulukuausi*" ("Baloma; The Spirits of the Dead," in *Magic, Science and Religion and Other Essays* [reprint; New York, 1954], pp. 153-54). The Balinese *leyak* has been cited as a werewolf but is better classified as a ghoul (see Jan Lodewijk Swellengrebel, *Bali: Studies in Life, Thought, and Ritual* [The Hague, 1960], p. 51).

[22] Cf. Malinowski: "It must be noted that the grave was in olden days situated in the middle of the village, and that a close vigil was kept over it, having, among other motives, that of protecting the corpse from these female ghouls. Now that the grave is outside the village the vigil has had to be abandoned, and the *mulukuausi* can prey on the corpse as they like. There seems to be an association between the *mulukuausi* and the high trees on which they like to perch, so that the present site of burial, placed as it is right among the high trees of the grove (*weika*) surrounding each village, is especialy odious to natives" ("Baloma," p. 257, n. 8).

into a pig or large fish, the ghouls feast on it and try to feed it to their human neighbors in order to turn them into ghouls like themselves. The ancient Filipinos buried their dead under or close to the house so that they could keep watch over the grave and the appropriate sights, sounds, and smells of human habitation would make the ghouls leave the grave alone.

Other names by which the aswang as a carrion-eater is known among various Philippine cultural-linguistic groups are *balbal* among the Tagbanua, *busaw* as a corpse thief among the Bagobo, *kagkag* among the Romblomanon, *segben* as a corpse thief among the East Visayan, and *wirwir* among the Apayao.

I have done a paper on Philippine social patterns sired by beliefs concerning ghouls,[23] and I will here just briefly sum up my findings and add a few other observations.

Since the beliefs about ghouls are associated with death, the final and most poignant episode in human experience, these beliefs help explain a number of details in Philippine culture. Funeral parlors in many modern Filipino communities, especially where there is electricity, provide blazing lights over and around the bier all

---

Also cf. Cole of the Andamanese: "The corpse is laid out in the hut, where it is visited by mourners, each smeared over with clay.....

"The head of the deceased is shaved, the body is painted with alternate lines of red and gray clay, the arms and legs are drawn close to the body, and the corpse is placed in a tree, or is buried wit head facing east. Various objects are placed by the grave, a fire is started nearby, taboo signs are erected, and the camp and vicinity are deserted during the period of mourning.

"When it is believed that the flesh has fallen from the bones the men smear their bodies with clay and return to the grave. The bones are dug up; the skull and jaw are covered with red paint and placed in a net bag which is worn for a time by the spouse. Leg and arm bones are painted also and placed in the roofs of the huts ..." (*Peoples of Malaysia*, p. 65). It seems reasonable to infer that the bright red paint, resembling as it does the color of fire, is intended to frighten off ghouls. Elsewhere, Cole says about the mortuary customs of the Semang of Malaya: "Friends and relatives wail but straightway start digging a grave and dispose of the corpse as quickly as possible" (*ibid.*, p. 66).

[23] *Western Folklore*, XXVII (July, 1968), 184-190.

day and all night. An oil lamp is kept burning in almost every Philippine home in remote communities all night, and many disastrous fires have started from this practice because the typical building materials in the villages are the highly inflammable bamboo, nipa, and thatch.[24]

Where other peoples are generally solemn and reserved at mortuary vigils, Filipinos are, as a number of Spanish chroniclers reported, quite noisy. At their vigils many Filipinos still sing, play parlor games, and feed large numbers of guests. In Bulacan, at the house where a dead man lay in state, the visitors were fed for three days before the burial, and three carabaos, half a dozen pigs, and 250 chickens were killed to feed them.

Fear that the ghoul may come and spirit the corpse away and kill the relatives as well explains why in many tradition-bound villages the family immediately desert or burn down their home and leave the locality when a member dies, no matter how new the house and how productive the clearing. This pattern has helped worsen the country's deforestation problems, although deforestation has in turn doubtless also been exacerbated by the fact that a clearing becomes less fruitful after a few seasons without crop rotation and adequate farm tools. The wasteful slash-and-burn type of tillage that has further denuded many rich forest areas in the country may very well have its roots in the belief that ghouls have material existence. This need to suddenly abandon one's domicile has discouraged rural Filipinos from building for permanence, using bamboo and thatch instead of stone for their buildings—although to be sure, homes built of these light materials are more suitable for the tropics, too.

The belief that ghouls were scared off by noise and loud talking may have contributed to the vociferousness of Filipinos when in groups. Coller found that radios which the Cooperative for American Relief Everywhere

---

[24] The title story in N. V. M. Gonzalez's *Seven Hills Away* (Denver, 1947) centers on the consequences of one such fire.

(CARE) had donated to isolated Philippine rural villages to spread helpful information where periodicals could not be had were often used to make "entertaining noises" at public gatherings instead of to receive information:

> In some social situations, it appeared that the sole function of the radio was to furnish a human-like noise as a background for an engrossing activity. An urban example is that of the college student who is habituated to studying with a radio accompaniment.
>
> In every instance where a similar situation occurred in the barrios, there was a large, group social activity taking place. At a wedding, for example, while the reception activities were in full blossom, the radio was placed on a table near the center of the room. However, the program was a somewhat indistinct sermon given in English by an evangelistic preacher. The volume of the radio was high although the separate words were not clear. No one moved to change the program nor to shut off the radio. Its "noise" was apparently a welcome addition to the wedding reception. An almost similar case occurred in another barrio when a large group of adults gathered to play bingo. Again the radio blared in the background with no one apparently caring about the specific programs.[25]

It is often quite easy to spot groups of Filipino students abroad because they are usually the most boisterous at gatherings. Filipino art forms like television shows, radio plays, and stage presentations seldom have quiet moments.

---

[25] Richard P. Coller, "Social Effects of Donated Radios on Barrio Life," Community Development Research Council Study Series no. 11 (mimeographed; University of the Philippines, 1961), p. 65.

The Filipinos's spicy cuisine can be largely explained by the country's proximity to the spice islands and to the real utility of spices for preserving food in the humid tropics before artificial refrigeration became possible. But it is also partly a function of the belief that vinegar, salt, and spices are considered as countermeasures against ghouls. The belief that ghouls return for those who attended the mortuary rites for the dead explains why the latter go back to the house of the bereaved to have their foreheads rubbed down with vinegar. The Filipino's habit of promiscuously spitting in public places may have been derived from his ancestors' custom of chewing aromatic betel the juice of which was believed effective in scaring off the aswang creatures as one went about his daily chores or walked in the woods. His habit of urinating in parks or at the roadsides, especially where there are no privies, was born of his belief that salt, such as that in urine, could drive the aswang away. His fondness for displaying metal objects on his person, including amulets, bladed weapons, and firearms, does not necessarily indicate a warlike nature; it can be more appropriately explained by the fact that these appurtenances were once thought to be effective countermeasures against the aswang, and the custom of carrying weapons even in public buildings has persisted to this day. Social habits and attitudes born of fear die hard.

A fresh insight into Philippine society can thus be gained from a knowledge of the folk beliefs concerning the aswang creatures.

Accounts About Aswang Creatures

THE FOLLOWING FOLK MATERIAL centers around the five types of aswang described previously and includes material about aswang that cannot be conveniently typed. These were all contributed by students in Philippine and European mythology at the University of the East. The students took the material down from informants or in some cases recorded them from memory and then wrote out their reports on 5 x 8 cards. That so much material could be had so quickly, even not counting the material that had to be left out, which was almost equal in volume to what appears here, is indicative of the amount and currency of aswang literature in Philippine society. Consisting of upperclassmen, the students had just completed a survey of Philippine lower mythology. A good number of them were enrolled in the preparatory medical curriculum.

Under each major aswang category the material is here arranged by geographical setting as indicated by the contributor's source, from Northern Luzon to Southern Mindanao and from east to west in the case of the Visayan material. It may be noted that we're reconteur and contributor came from different linguistic regions in the country, either English or the trade languages like Iloko and Tagalog served as the communication medium.

I wish to acknowledge the valuable help of the following consultants who checked the vernacular texts with the English translations, particularly the authenticity of the texts: Fred Buyagao, for Ifugao; Leticia E. Cabang, Eva Lim-Pascual, Felix D. Ricafort, and Amelia V. Solomon, for Iloko; Juanita F. Calimlim, Felicidad M. Cayme, Susan B. Geronimo, and Flory Y. Malicdem, for Pangasinan; Concepcion H. Abregunda, Eufracia L. Aledo, Amparo B. Aliazas, Leticia R. Cunanan, Inez A. Medado, Bienvenido G. Nacorda, Dionisio S. Salazar, and Belen L. Vitor, for Tagalog; Julieta G. Amaranto, Fe M. Jaymalin, Daniel L. Manalang, Salvador T. Rodulfo, and Leticia M. Tabuena, for Bikol, Catanduanes, and Sorsogon; Corazon A. Saavedra and Estrella N. Sotto, for Waray; Vicente A. Arbole, Victor M. Barroso, Fe V. Brilliantes, Mars T. Edillor, Florcita G. Tabuena, and Melodia F. Tesalona, for Cebu-Visayan; Salvador G. Blancia, Ricardo P. Garcia, Rita J. Jimenez, and Gloria M. Marañon, for Hiligaynon; and Maria V. Moreno, for Kiniray-a.

To Dr. Juan R. Francisco, former dean of the University of the Philippines College in Tarlac, go my thanks for the idea, subsequently approved by the Philippine Folklore Society, that texts and translations of accounts about the aswang creatures should be added to my description of these creatures appearing as part I of this book; and to Mauro Garcia, scholar, editor, and friend, many *salamat* for his putting the manuscript in order for the press.

I take the blame, however, for any error that may have persisted and for any other shortcomings of the effort.

Thanks are due, finally, to Amelita A. Galang, Corazon Ganacias, Nenita Ocampo, Bienvenida Tan, Letty Lokett, and Bella M. Prudencio for their excellent secretarial services.

Ghoul Legends

1. [THE *UMANGOB*][26]
Ifugao Text

*Wada han pangat nadan Ifugao hidin kanaman an
ihangdel da nan nateh nan daulon ya nun-apoy dah nan nunlikkodan. Wada-day tatagon maniboh nan apoy ta adi mate, te
tumakut dah nan umangob. Ya wada han itanom dan munda-
dala an tanum (dongla) hinan nunlikkodan te kulogon da un
tumakut nan umangob i-di-ye.*

*Hay tibo na ya kay ong-nga-ong-ngal an kahon
mangmangiti't an umalih nan hilong ta alana nan o-ongal an
kimong nan takle ya nan kuhin nan nate. Adi na dap-dapaon
nan udum an hi adol nan nate nu bukon nan ong-ngal an
kimong ya abu ya maid ha udum tumaktana nu bokon nan
apuy ya nan dongla mu mabalin an la-u-hana da-tuwe te kay
kilat an mange.*

There is an old custom among the Ifugao to hang
their dead under the house and build fires around it.
People keep vigil and keep all the fires alive, for they
are afraid of the *umangob*.

---

[26] Contributed by Aida B. Ayong, an Ifugao, writing about her recollec-
tions of beliefs in an Ifugao community.

1

They also plant a crimson herb, *dongla*, around the house, for it is believed that the *umangob* is afraid of it. It looks like a big black police dog that comes at night to steal the big toes and the thumbs of the corpse. It does not touch any other part of the corpse except the big toes and the thumbs.

It is not afraid of any other thing except the dongla and live fire. But it can pass through these, for it moves like lightning.

2. [FEAST IN A CEMETERY][27]
Iloko Text

Kuna ni Apongko ket maysa kano nga agsipnget idi aga-wid idiay barriomi, nagna idiay kampusanto. Idi nakaguduat dalannan, nakakita it uppat a tao nga agap-apa a mangman-gan. Adda ulo a naiparabaw idiay pantion ngem saanna nga indandaneng. Aw-awisen da kano ngem timmaray. Idi maka-danon idiay balay, nagbissag ta nalagip na daydi kasinsinna nga impumpunda iti nabiit.

My grandfather said that one day at sunset, while he was going home to our barrio, he passed through the cemetery. Halfway through, he saw four individuals quarreling at their meal. A head was on a tomb but he did not give it any significance. They invited him to join them but he ran away. When he got home his face was very pale because he remembered that his cousin had been buried recently.

---

[27] Contributed by Wigberto N. Corpuz, from Agno, Pangasinan, who had it from Eleanor Narvaiz Corpuz, an elementary schoolteacher from Tidog, Agno, who in turn had it from Josefa Nitafan Corpuz, of the same community.

3. [HOW A GHOUL GETS A CORPSE][28]
Tagalog Text

Noong araw, ang mga Bulakeño ay naniniwala na ang aswang ay dumarating pag may patay na nakaburol. Ito ang dahilan ng kanilang pagbabantay sa patay, lalong lalo na ang paglalamay na hindi nila nakakaligtaan.

Ayon sa kanila, ang aswang ay nakararating sa lugar na pinagbuburulan nang wala silang malay. Hindi pa sila nakakakita kung ano ang itsura nito, kaya hindi sila nakatitiyak kung ito'y ispirito lamang.

Ayon sa mga nakasaksi, ang patay ay sinusubuan ng aswang ng asoge. At hindi magtatagal ang patay ay tatayo, maglalakad, at susunod sa sinumang nagsubo sa kanya. Ito ang paraan ng aswang para niya makuha ang patay.

Ang nangyari sa aming kapitbahay noong araw ay isang magandang halimbawa. Ang kanyang asawa ay namatay, at nang sumapit ang gabi at nang ang lahat ng bisita ay nakauwi na, siya lamang ang natira. Upang makatiyak na hindi lalapitan ng aswang ang patay, siya ay tumabi dito, niyakap ito, at natulog.

In the old days the Bulakeños believed that the aswang usually came when the dead was lying in state. That is why they watch the dead and especially do not forget to keep vigil.

According to them, the aswang usually comes to a wake without their knowledge. They have never seen what it looks like, so they are not sure if it is merely a spirit.

According to witnesses, the dead body is given asoge by the aswang directly in the mouth, and a few minutes later he will stand, walk, and follow the one who gave it to him. This is how the aswang is able to get the corpse.

---

[28] Contributed by Iniceta Soriano, from San Miguel, Bulacan, who collected it from Urbana Cruz, a housekeeper from the same town.

3

What happened to our former neighbor is a good example. His wife died, and after all the visitors had gone home, he alone was left with her corpse. In order to make sure that the aswang couldn't get near his wife, he lay down beside the corpse, embraced it, and slept.

4. [A DOGLIKE GHOUL][29]
Tagalog Text

Nang magkasakit ang lolo ko, ay isang itim na asong may taas na apat na talampakan at may malalaking taingang pumapagaspas kapag siya'y lumalakad at umakyat sa bahay, dinilaan ang lolo ko, at ang lolo ko ay namatay.

When my grandfather became ill, a black dog, four feet tall and with big ears that flapped as it walked, came up to the house and licked my grandfather, and my grandfather died.

5. [THE CORPSE THIEF][30]
Sorsogon Text

Cang ako nasa hababa pang grado igwa duman ning sarong lalake sa samuya na piga tugod tugodan na sarong aswang. Ang bangkay perming pigabantayan ning marinas, sa takot na cuwaon ito. Sarong banggui naguimata cami sa yayat ning mga ayam. Saro sa cairiba me natultul pa ang isip na guiromduman ang aswang, buda cang oras mismo na ito nagsirip sa sirong kan harong. Nakahiling sinda ning lalake. Cang pagpahara ninda, buda cang pagbukoda nawara so lalake. Pero an nahiling sarong daculang ayam. Pigbucod ninda so ayam na dagos nawara sa caduluman.

[29] Contributed by Miguel H. Benedicto, from Pasay City, who had it from Teresita Estocado, from San Isidro, Bulusan, Sorsogon.

[30] Contributed by Ma. Yolanda R. Borjal, of Virac, Catanduanes, who had it from Salvacion R. Borjal, a government employee from Gubat, Sorsogon.

When I was in the lower grades, there lived in our town a man believed to be an aswang. Corpses were always carefully watched for fear that he would spirit them away. One night during a wake, dogs began barking and howling. Someone with presence of mind remembered the aswang and at once decided to look under the house. They saw a man. When they drove him away and ran after him, they found nobody but a big dog. They ran after the dog, but it disappeared in the dark.

6. [TYING AN ASWANG][31]
Bikol Text

Mahapdos an lolo co. Awat na namo imparababolong sa doctor pero diri man naayad. May pera na kagabi na diri nacaturog nan nagpapanaalinpasay.

Sayo caadlao may nacapagnoticia na basi god ugaring inaasuwang an lolo niyo: "Con gusto mo macierto bantayan mo doon sa gabi pero diri ca magpasicop sin suna cay diri mo yuon maiimod."

Cuinagab-ihan binantayan ni Sandy an asuwang: Naawat siya sin katulat. Taod-taod umabot na an asuwang. Hinapot siya con awat na doon. Sinimbag ni Sandy na awat na siya nan tinagan niya si lugar an asuwang. Pagcuitay san asuwang sa salog, pinuropotan ni Sandy sin lubid nan hinigot sa harigi.

Pero san plaslaitan na niya, palapa ugaring san lubi ang nagagacot sa harigi.

Pagcaaga nacadto si Sandy sa padi para umayo danon. Tinagan siya sin benditado na cordon na mao an ihihigot niya sa asuwang. Pira cagabi wara pagbuelta an asuwang. Pagcatapos sin duwa casemana yuon na naman an asuwang.

---

[31] Contributed by Harold G. Fajardo, from Gubat, Sorsogon, who had it from Felicitas Panuga, who heard it years before.

5

Maoman guihapon ang hapot sa canya. Pagcuitay san
asuwang hinigutan tulos ni Sandy san cordon.

Wara pacahiro an asuwang. San plaslaitan ni Sandy an
asuwang sayo man hamoc ngayon na gurang na tawo, an
nagestar sa harani na baryo. Nacuimalooy an gurang na pata-
wadon na siya cay diri na man siya maulit nan bobolangon
niya an mahapdos.

Tuminogot si Sandy. Pagcaaga binolong san gurang an
mahapdos asin siya uminayad.

My grandfather was sick. He had been under the
physician's care for a long time but had not recovered.
For several nights he could not sleep and was uneasy.

One day someone said that it could be that my
grandfather was being visited by the aswang, saying: "If
you want to be sure, watch for the aswang tonight, but
be sure you don't see any light before twilight or else
you won't see him."

Night came. Sandy watched for the aswang. He waited for a long time. Later the aswang arrived and asked
whether Sandy had long been there. Sandy replied that
he had long been there and gave way to the aswang. As
the aswang clung underneath, Sandy bound him and
tied him to a post.

But when he switched on his flashlight, he saw a coconut trunk tied to the post.

The following morning Sandy went to the priest to
ask for advice. The priest gave him a blessed cord to tie
the aswang. For several nights the aswang didn't return.
Then after two weeks it came. The same queries were
asked. When the aswang clung underneath the house,
Sandy at once tied it with the cord.

The aswang was unable to move. When Sandy
switched on his flashlight, it was just an old man who
lived in a neighboring barrio. The old man begged for
mercy and that he be set free, for he wouldn't do it
again and would cure the sick man.

Sandy consented. The following morning the old
man cured the sick man. Then he was relieved of his illness.

6

7. [BANANA TRUNK FOR A CORPSE][32]
Tagalog Text

*May isang tao sa amin na bigla na lamang nagkasakit.
Bawat oras ay tumataas ang kanyang lagnat. Tumawag ang
asawa niya ng albularyo. Ngunit ilang saglit bago dumating
ang albularyo, ang taong iyon ay namatay. Pagkakita ng albularyo sa bangkay ay kanyang sinabi sa asawa nito na hindi
iyon and kanyang asawa. Ang asawa daw niya ay nasa kamay
ng mga aswang. Kaagad silang nagpunta sa pook na sinabi
ng albularyo. Ang lalaki ay nadatnan nilang papatayin na ng
mga aswang upang kainin. Nang makita ng mga aswang ang
mga tao, sila ay tumakas. At hindi na napatay ng mga
aswang ang lalaki. Nang sila'y bumalik sa kanilang bahay,
isang tinibang saging ang kanilang nakita sa halip na
bangkay na kanilang iniwan.*

There was a man in our place who suddenly sick-
ened. Every hour his fever rose. His wife called an *albularyo*. But a few moments before the arrival of the albularyo, the man died. When the albularyo saw the dead
man, he told the widow that that was not her husband
and that her husband was in the hands of the aswang.
They rushed to the place the albularyo indicated and
they arrived just in time, when the aswang were about
to kill her husband and eat him. The aswang fled when
they saw them coming. When they returned to the
house of the man, they found a banana trunk in place of
the corpse.

[32] Contributed by Miguel H. Benedicto, from Pasay City, who collected it
from Arsenio E. Benedicto, a retired government employee from Villadolid,
Negros Occidental.

8. [THE UMBRELLA-LIKE ASWANG][33]
Kiniray-a Text

Ang amigo ko nga si Edgar, tambok nga tao sa amon banwa, ang nag-istorya sa akon cadya.

Ca nga pauli tana naglaktud tana sa patyo. Mga pira ca metro pa lang tana sa patyo sang maagyan kana cang hubot. Dagiton raad tana pero ginbutong na ang anang kutsilyo sa ana ulo ug iwaswas. Tapos, nagpalagyo tana sa mga kahoy kag nagbali cang sanga nga damo duro ang si-it. Pagdagit liwan sang hubot gin paspas na cang si-it. Nagpalagyo ang hubot kay nahadlok gali cang si-it.

Ko-on ni Edgar canakon na ang hubot nahadlok gali cang si-it, cag con may metal ca nga kuarta indi siya makadara canimo.

My friend Edgar, a big, stout man in our town, told me this story.

Going home, he decided to take a shortcut across the cemetery. He was only a few meters from the cemetery when an umbrella-like creature called *hobot* passed over his head. The hobot tried to pull him up but he shook his knife over his head to ward it off. Then Edgar ran to the bushes and broke off a thorny branch from a tree. When the hobot made another attack, he smashed at it with the thorny branch several times. The hobot flew away and cried in pain.

Edgar told me it was an aswang in the form of a hobot. He also said that the hobot is afraid of thorns, and if you have coins in your pocket, it cannot pull you up.

---

[33] Contributed by Regino V. Hofileña, from San Jose, Antique, who had it from Edgar Magbanua, an employee from the same town.

8

9. [FLIGHT ON A WAKWAK'S BACK][34]
Cebu-Visayan Text

Dunay usa ka lalaki nga nagpuyo sa balay. Usa ka hapon may wakwak nag-ingun, "Wak-wak-wak." Nitubag ang lalaki sa balay, "Mouban ko." Dayon ta-od ta-od diha na ang dalaga. Ni-ingun nga, "Dali na! Molakaw na ta!" Nanaog sila sa balay, hinsakay ang lalaki sa wakwak, lupad sila. Layu na ka-ayo sila, nakita sa lalaki na dunay balay nga daghang tawo. Ang mga tawo naghilak sa balay, nagingun ang dalaga, "Ibilin lang ka dinhi sa taas sa lubi." Ni lupad ang wakwak. Niadto sa balay, siging hilak ang mga tawo, mi sulud ang wakwak, guikuha niya ang patay. Ang mga tawo wala mahibalo na ang patay guikuha sa wakwak ug guidala sa wakwak ang patay sa taas sa lubi. Guicarga sa lalaki ang patay sa likod niya ug dayon nisakay ang lalaki sa wakwak ug nilupad sila. Layu na, wala makahibalo, ang lalaki kung asan'g lugar, nakaabot sila sa bahay sa wakwak. Guibutang ang patay sa balay, guitawag sa dalaga ang iyang nanay, "Nay, ania na kami, naay akong dala." Paggawas sa nanay nakita ang lalaki. "O, kinsa ang imong kauban?" Nitubag ang dalaga, "Akong migo, Nay." Guipaluto ang patay sa iyang nanay, nahadlok ang lalaki, pero wala lang siya magbanha. Tapos naluto, na mingtawag ang nanay, "Kaon na." Guitawag ang lalaki sa babai, "Kaon na." Unya wala mukaon ang lalaki, natulog ang lalaki. Pakabuntag, guapo na ang balay sa wakwak. Nilakaw ang lalaki nagpalit ug tambal, guibutang niya ang tambal sa pagkaon. Pagkahuman nagkaun ang dalaga ug ang iyang mama, nagsuka sila. Pulus langam gagmay, naluya sila, dayun naulian di na sila makalupad pagkagabi, kay nigawas na ang langam gagmay, di na sila wakwak. Tapos mag-asawa ang dalaga at ang lalaki.

There was a boy who was staying home. One afternoon there was a wakwak who said, "Wak-wak-wak."

[34] Contributed by Elizabeth Go, from Zamboanga City, who collected it from Lingling Labisto, of Pagadian, Zamboanga del Sur, who in turn had it from Balit, farmer, of the same town.

9

The boy answered from the house, "I want to go with you." Suddenly a young woman appeared. She said, "Hurry up! Let's go." They went down from the house, the boy rode on the wakwak, and they flew. When they got very far, the boy saw a house with many people. The people were crying, and the wakwak said, "Stay here on top of this coconut tree." Then the wakwak flew away. She went to the house. The people kept on crying inside the house. The wakwak entered the house, took the dead. But the people did not know that the dead had been taken away by the wakwak and carried to the top of the coconut tree. The boy carried the dead on his back, now he rode on the wakwak. Then they flew away. Far away, nobody knows, even the boy, where it was, they reached the house of the wakwak. The dead they placed inside the house. The young woman called her mother, "Ma! We are here. I brought something." When the mother came out, she saw the boy. "Oh, who is with you?" The young woman answered, "My friend, Ma." She had her mother cook the dead, the boy was frightened, but he did not mind it. When everything was cooked, the mother called, "Let's eat." The young lady called to the boy, "Let's eat." Now the boy did not want to eat; he went to sleep. In the morning the house of the wakwak had become very beautiful; the boy took a walk and bought some medicine and placed it on the food. When the young woman and her mother finished eating their food, they vomited. All that came out were small birds, and they were very tired, and they could not fly anymore at night. Because the small birds were out of their body, they were not wakwak any more. Later the boy and the young lady got married.

Vampire Legends

10. [A BLOOD-DRINKING ASWANG][35]
Sorsogon Text

*Can ako saday pang aqui may nagiroc sa harani sa
samuyang harong na babaye na sa pagtubod cang mga tawo
sarong aswang. Ang sacong ama na sanitary inspector dai
nagtutubod sa aswang.*

*Sarong aldao ang canatad me naghelang. Lambang miem-
bro can pamilya nacabantay sa nagahelang na babaye nin
husay, sa pagtubod na igwang aswang. Sarong banggi can
ang gabos nacapamanggi na, ang sarong bantay nagkurahaw
na may babaye sa sirong. Ang mga lalake nagdaralagan sa
ibaba ta dadacupon si aswang. Ang babaye napiritan na
magdulag kaya dai na naguibo so plano nia na sopsopon so
dugo kan nagahelang na babaye. Kaya poon caidto so aswang
dai na nahiling sa samong canatad sagcod ngonian.*

When I was a young girl there lived, near our house,
a woman believed to be an aswang. My father, a sanitary inspector, did not believe in aswang.

[35] Contributed by Ma. Yolanda R. Borjal, from Virac, Catanduanes, who had
it from Salvacion R. Borjal, a government employee from Gubat, Sorsogon.

One day a neighbor got sick. Every member of the family watched her very carefully because of the supposed aswang. One night when everyone was at supper, someone shouted that there was a woman under the [sick woman's] house. The men ran down to catch her. The woman had to escape and failed in her desire to suck the blood of the sick woman. From that time on that aswang was not seen in our neighborhood again.

11. [A HOUSE FULL OF VAMPIRES][36]
Tagalog Text

May isang sundalo na napaligaw sa Dueñas, isang barrio sa Iloilo. Dahil sa mayroon siyang kakilala doon na ang pangalan ay Sario, doon siya nakituloy. "Sario, Sario, si Ruben ito, ang kaibigan mong sundalo. Maari bang makitulog, dahil sa ginabi ako sa daan?" Siya naman ay pinatuloy at dinala sa nag-iisang silid sa bahay. Napansin niya na maraming tao sa bahay ni Sario. "Marami pala kayong bisita, nakakahiya," ang sabi ng sundalo. "Mga kaibigan iyan ni nanay. Mamaya lang, aalis na sila," ang sagot naman ni Sario. Nang natutulog na si Ruben, bigla siyang nagising sa amoy na kakaiba at parang malansa. Nakarinig siya ng kaluskos sa kuwarto, pagkatapos ay may naramdaman siyang dumarapo sa kanya. Nakita niyang ito ay isang malaking paniki. Hinugot niya ang dala niyang gulok (itak) at sumigaw siya, "Ikaw, yawa ka, patiyon kita karon!" (Ikaw na demonyo ka, papatayin kita ngayon!) Pagkatapos, tinawag niya si Sario. Pagpasok ni Sario sa kuwarto, nawala and paniki at ang amoy. Lumabas na si Sario. Mayamaya'y naramdaman na naman ni Ruben na may dumikit sa katawan niyang parang matulis na karayom. Sumigaw siya at inilabas ang kanyang gulok. Pumasok uli si Sario sa kuwarto at ang sabi, "Nay, ayaw pagbinuang" (Nanay, huwag kang magluko-luko diyan). Natakot si Ruben

[36] Contributed by Immaculada B. Blancaflor, from Santa, Ilocos Sur, who gathered it from Teofista Bumagat, a housemaid from Dueñas, Iloilo.

kaya naisipan niyang umalis sa bahay na yaon. Kabilugan ang buwan. Sa pamamagitan ng liwanag nito ay nakita niya paglabas sa kuwarto, sa sala, ang maraming katawang walang mga ulo at putol mula baywang. Kumuha siya ng asin at nilagyan niya ang lahat ng putol na katawan. Pagkatapos, umalis si Ruben sa bahay. Nakituloy siya sa ibang bahay at doon niya nalaman na ang nanay ni Sario ay siyang pinuno ng mga aswang sa Barrio Dueñas at doon sa bahay nila Sario sila nagpupulong.

～⁊

There was a soldier who got lost in Dueñas, a barrio in Iloilo. Because he knew someone there named Sario, he decided to go to Sario's house. "Sario, Sario, this is your soldier friend Ruben. May I sleep here for the night?" He was let in and led into the only room in Sario's house. He noticed that there were many people in the house. "I did not know you had many visitors. It is very embarrassing," said the soldier. "They are friends of my mother, and by and by they will leave," answered Sario. When Ruben was asleep, he was suddenly awakened by a peculiar smell. He heard movements in the room and then he felt something touching him. He saw that it was a big bat. He pulled out his bolo and shouted, "You devil, I will kill you!" Then he called Sario. When Sario came into the room, the bat and the smell disappeared. Sario left the room. After a while, Ruben again felt something touching his body. It felt like the tip of a sharp needle. He shouted and brought out his bolo. Sario came to the room again and said, "Mother, don't fool around here." Ruben got scared and he decided to leave the house. The moon was full and bright as he came out of his room. By its light he saw bodies in the sala, cut through the waist with no heads. He hurriedly took salt and sprinkled it on all the cut bodies. Then Ruben left the house. He decided to spend the rest of the night in another house and there he learned that the mother of Sario was the head of the aswang in Barrio Dueñas, and it was in Sario's house that the aswang periodically met.

12. [THE *MARANHIG*][37]
Hiligaynon Text

Ang tigulang sa lugar nga dia ay kilala nga maranhig.
Indi dia mapatay kon wara ti pamilya ang magsunod ca a-
nang birtud. Kon magpakitlu-oy tana nga kuptan ang ana na
birtud malabas ang anang laway nga wara ti pu-ot hasta ma-
abut sa lupa. Ang mga bata na cadia nga lalaki nakapanga-
sawa sa iba nga probinsiya. Ang mga dalaga tana nga bata
nagala-on kag indi makapangasawa kon indi ang isara
cananda mag-ako sa anang tatay. Duro ang nagmamasakit
nga mga tao nga nagahambal cananda.

An old man from a distant barrio in one of our
towns is known throughout as a *maranhig*. This man is
old and cannot die unless someone in his family inherits
his power. Whenever he begs his children to take his
power, saliva comes out of his mouth and reaches down
to the ground. The saliva is long like a rope and sticky.
His sons married women from outside the province who
did not know about their sickness. His daughters have
become spinsters and cannot marry unless one of them
inherits her father's power.

Only one in the family will become a maranhig and
will do as he does. The old man used to make those
who talked about them sick.

---

[37] Contributed by Regino V. Hofileña, from San Jose, Antique, who had it
from Joaquin de los Santos, tuba gatherer from Supa, San Jose.

13. [A MAN'S FIGHT WITH AN ASWANG][38]
Hiligaynon Text

"Segun sa akon tiyo nakaagi siya sang matuod nga
pagpakig-away batok sa aswang," sugid ni Mercy sa akon.

"Tuod-tuod mo gid nga tiyo?" ang pamangkot ko sa iya.

"Aba, hu-o. Nahibaluan mo batasan namon ang mag-
sugilanon bag-o magtulog sa gab-i. Isa sang iya sugilanon
amo ang natuñgod sang iya pagpakigsumpong sa aswang.
Wala siya nagalipod kay bisan ang akon mga ginikanan
nakahibalo man gani."

"Nagapati ka man bala sa aswang?" ang akon pamangkot.

"Aba, hu-o."

"Ti kon amo abi sugiri ako," siling ko sa iya.

"Sang pagbakasyon sadto sang akon tiyo sa Antique
nakapañgaluyag siya sang isa kamagayon nga lin-ay didto.
Madamo ang nagsiling nga aswang kuno pero wala ugaling
siya magpati. Daw indi niya napatihan kung ano katahum
niya ugaling isa lang ka aswang. Nagpadayon siya pangluyag
tubtob nga napahando niya ang lin-ay. Pagkatapos nadunggan sang lin-ay nga kalaslon gali ang akon tiyo sa amon
banwa. Isa ka gab-i sang maghalin siya pamasyar sa balay
sang babae, hinali lamang siya nga nilambatan sa dalanon
sang isa ka tigulang nga babae. Makahaladlok kuno ang
dagway kag malaba ang buhok. Pagkatapos hinamag siya kag
ginkuga. Nagbato siya pero kakusog sang amo nga tigulang.
Labot pa masyado kadanlog sang iya lawas kag bisan ang iya
buhok. Dumdom sang akon tiyo nga katapusan na niya sang
hindi niya nga nadakpan ang kumalagko sang tigulang. Ubos
kusog niya nga kinagat. Wala gid niya pagbuy-i kon wala
mag-ampo ang tigulang kag ginsaran siya nga sa baylo sang
iya kaluwasan amo ang lanahan nga ginasipit niya sa iya
ilok. Ginbaton naman sang akon tiyo ang condisyon.

[38] Contributed by Evelyn Lorenzo, from Mexico, Pampanga, who collected
it from Mercy Bantilla, a college graduate from Negros Occidental.

"Nakita ko gid ang botelya sang lanahan nga may unod nga kahoy-kahoy," ang padayon niya. Ang siling niya nga segun sa tigulang maga-awas ang lana kon may makasaka nga ginasugid nga aswang sa balay."

"Nakita mo gid ang botelya?" ang pamangkot ko.

"Aba, hu-o. Daw amo ini kadako kag may mga panit sang kahoy sa sulod sang lanahan. Apang sang pagkakita ko sang lanahan tunga na lang ang unod."

"Nga-a ano ang natabo nga nagtunga na lang," ang sabat ko.

"Ti kay man ginagamit man sang akon tiyo sa sakit sang tiyan, sakit ulo kag iban pa nga masakit. Siling niya pa gid nga maynakadkadto sa ila balay sang isa sina ka adlaw nga manug-otan. Nakasaka na siya sa balay pero wala pa niya paghukasa ang iya turban kay gali puno sang pinalian sang pilas. Madamo ang nagsiling nga aswang kuno adto, segun sa akon tiyo nag-awas ang lanahan sang pagsulod sang manugotan sa ila balay."

"According to my uncle he had a personal experience fighting with an aswang," Mercy told me.

"A close uncle of yours?" I asked her.

"O, yes. Well, you see, we used to tell stories before we went to bed at night. And one of his stories was about his fight with an aswang, a real aswang. I know my uncle did not make up the story because my parents knew his experience too."

"Do you believe in the aswang?" I interpreted her.

"O, yes I do."

"Okay, go on with the story," I told her.

"My uncle happened to court a lovely girl from Antique when he once had his vacation there. Many told him that she was an aswang but he would not listen. He could not believe that such a beauty could be an aswang. He kept on courting her until she gave him her 'Yes.' After that, it happened that the girl learned from others that my uncle was already engaged to be married to someone else from our town. Then one night on his

17

way home not far from the girl's house after he had visited her, he saw an old, ugly, long-haired woman. Suddenly she grabbed his neck and tried to strangle him. He desperately fought back but to no avail. He could not match her strength, and besides her body and even her hair were very slippery. He thought it would be his end until he took hold of her thumb and bit it vigorously till she begged for mercy. She promised to give him a bottle of oil she kept under her armpit if he set her free. He took the bargain and had the bottle of oil.

"I have personally seen this bottle of oil," Mercy continued. "It was a very small bottle, and besides the oil in it you could see pieces of tree bark also. He said that according to the old woman the oil would overflow from the bottle if someone happened to come inside your house who was an aswang."

"Did you really see the bottle?" I asked her.

"O, yes. It was that big and with pieces of bark of trees mixed with the oil. But when I saw it, the oil was only that much."

"How come it was only that much then?" I asked her.

"Well, you see, my uncle used it for stomachache, headache, and other minor illnesses. He also said that one day a woman peddling vegetables went up into the house of my uncle. This woman had many scars all over her body, even on her head. That is why she always wore a bandanna. Many suspected her of being an aswang and you know, according to my uncle, the oil overflowed when this person entered his house."

Weredog Legends

14. [ASWANG WHO KILLS WITH HER HAIR][39]
Tagalog Text

Dito sa barrio ng Francis, Calumpit, Bulacan, ay may lumalabas na aswang tuwing kabilugan ng buwan. Ayon sa mga nakakakita, ito ay isang babaing maputi at mahaba ang buhok. Ang kanyang pamamaraan ng pagpatay ay ganito: kapag ang kanyang biktima ay malapit na sa kanya, ang kanyang malagong buhok ay pilit na ipapasok sa butas ng ilong at bibig ng biktima upang ito ay hindi makahinga.

Here in the barrio of Francis, Calumpit, Bulacan, an aswang appears every full moon. Those who have seen her say she is a tall, fair girl with long hair. Her method of killing is like this: when her victim is near her, she forcibly inserts her long hair into the nostrils and mouth of the victim so that he will be choked to death.

---

[39] Contributed by Wilfredo Mananquil, from Calumpit, Bulacan, who had it from Carlos Mananquil, of the same town.

15. [A LONG-HAIRED HUNCHBACK][40]
Tagalog Text

Nagtaguan kami. Marahil ika-12 ng gabi nang kami'y makatapos. Tinawag ko si Eduardo upang tingnan yaong bagay na nakita ko sa silong ng aming bahay. Pagkatapos sinabi ko, "Eduardo, Eduardo, tingan mo yaong nasa silong ng bahay." "Asan? Asan?" sabi naman ni Eduardo. "Oo nga, ano?" Nang makita niya ang isang matandang may mahabang buhok at waring kuba at pabalik-balik na lumalakad, sinabi ko kay Eduardo, "Tumakbo tayo nang mabilis." Ngunit ayaw niya. Pinikit ko ang aking mga mata at saka tumakbo nang mabilis na mabilis. Nang dumating ako sa amin, ako'y nahiga. Tapos narinig ko si Eduardo na tumatawag, "Ma! Ma!" Kami'y magkapit-bahay kaya ko siya narinig. Sabi ng nanay niya, "Ano bang batang ito? Maglalaro at pagkatapos ay tawag nga tawag nang akin."

Noong umaga itinanong ko sa kanila kung anong nangyari noong nagdaang gabi. Ang sagot ng bata, "Nang dumating ang Mama ko, biglang nawala ang matanda."

We had been playing hide-and-seek and now we were through. I think it was twelve midnight when we finished. Now I was holding on to Eduardo and then I said, "Eduardo, Eduardo, look at what's under the house." "Where? Where?" Eduardo asked. "Oh, yes, isn't it?" We saw an old man with very long hair and he was kind of hunchbacked and was walking back and forth. Then I said, "Let's run fast," but he didn't want to. So what I did was close my eyes and run fast, and when I reached home, went straight to bed. Then I could hear Eduardo calling, "Ma! Ma!" We were neighbors, that's why I heard him. His mother said, "What child is this? He goes out playing and then calls and calls."

---

[40] Contributed by Amelia E. Santos, of Brooke's Point, Palawan, who had it from Caridad Pajarillo, of San Juan, Rizal.

The next morning I asked him what happened the night before.

"Nothing. When my mother came it disappeared," was the child's relpy.

(CONTRIBUTOR'S NOTE: "Caridad Pajarillo was very excited in telling me her story. She thought it was funny although she said she was really scared when it happened years before.")

16. [THE PIG WITH REVERSIBLE ENDS][41]
Tagalog Text

Minsan, may nagpuntang tao sa bahay nina Nana Ineng upang mangutang ng bigas. Ngunit siya ay walang mai-pahiram na bigas. Pagkaalis noong tao ay nagkabukol sa kata-wan si Nana Ineng. Pinaghinalaan niya yaong tao, kaya kan-yang pinatawag. Ngunit sabi noong tao ay hindi siya aswang— ngunit pagkalaway noong tao kay Nana Ineng, ay nawala yaong bukol.

May pinuntahang bahay ang taong yaon at may dinatnan siyang maysakit. Pagkaalis noong tao may sumipot na pagkalaki-laking baboy na naninilong sa tapat ng hinihigaan ng maysakit. Ngayon, naghinala yaong ina noong bata doon sa tao, kayat tinaga nila yaong baboy at tinamaan sa pigi.

Pumunta siya sa bahay noong tao, at nakita niyang ito ay may napakalaking tagihawat.

Ngunit sa katunayan pala, ay ang pigi ng baboy ay siyang mukha, at ano mang sugat na magkaroon siya ay na-pag-aanyo niyang iba.

Nagkataon namang ang matanda palang yaon (ang ina ng bata) ay may nalalaman ding laban sa aswang, kayat pagbaba niya ng bahay ng tao ay binaliktad niya ang hagdanan (yari sa kawayan) noong bahay. Kaya namatay yaong taong pinaghinalaan nilang aswang.

Mula noon ay wala ng nangyari sa kanilang ganoon.

---

[41] Contributed by Zenaida M. Salcedo, from Calauag, Quezon, who had it from Leonila Cayme, of the same town.

A man once came to Nana Ineng's home and asked to borrow some rice. But she had no rice to lend. After the man left, a lump developed on Nana Ineng's body. She suspected the man and had him called. He denied that he had that—he was not aswang—but when he put some of his saliva on Nana Ineng, the lump disappeared.

The man visited a house and it happened that somebody there was sick. After he left, a very large pig went under the place where the patient was lying. Now the mother suspected the man, so she struck the pig's posterior with her bolo.

She went to the man's house and found that he had very large pimples.

But in fact, the posterior of the pig is his face, and he can change any cut that he has to something else (such as pimples).

It happened that the old woman (the child's mother) knew some countermeasures against the aswang, so as soon as she went down the stairs (made of bamboo) of the house, she turned it upside down, and suddenly the suspected man died.

From then on nothing of the kind happened in the locality.

17. [RIDE ON A PIG][42]
Tagalog Text

Pauwing hilo ang bise alkalde mula sa inuman nang makarinig siya ng tinig na nagsasabing, "Sakay na!" Isang napakalaking baboy ang nagsalita. At sapagka't siya ay lasing, sinakyan niya ang baboy na nalalaman ang kaniyang tinitirhan sa Baryo Binagbag. Nang siya ay bumaba, napansin

---

[42] Contributed by Alicia S. Sylva, of Makati, Rizal, who had it from Adelia Padilla, from Agdanganan, Quezon, who in turn heard it from Berto Monterey, a former vice mayor of the same town.

niyang suot ng baboy ang isa niyang asul na gomang tsine-las. Sa kaniyang malaking pagkatakot, nawala ang kaniyang pagkalasing at siya ay tumakbo. Nang balikan niya ang baboy upang barilin, ito ay nawala na.

❧

On his dizzy way home from a drinking session, the vice mayor heard a voice which said, "*Sakay na!* " (Get on!) It was a very huge pig that spoke. And because he was drunk, he rode the pig, which knew his house in Barrio Binagbag. When he got off, he noticed that the pig was wearing a blue rubber slipper [*sic*]. He became so afraid that his drunkenness was gone and he ran. When he returned to shoot the pig, it had been swallowed by the dark.

18. [A WEREDOG STABBED][43]
Bicol Text

Si Pay Blas nag-coma sa Pon-od. Solo lang na hinimo niya sa gilid san kaniya pasakay. Ini si Pay Blas may hapdos na pag-abot sa hapon siya gin tatakigan o ginpapanluya. Sayo sa gab-i, gin atake naman sin caniya hapdos kaya diri niya nakaon ang kaniya gin luto para sa kaniya panigabi. Gin puntalan niya sin mayad ang solo na portahan san balay asin pagkatapos nagtacod siya sin mosquitero para makaturog na. San mapiyong na hamoc siya may nabati siya na kaluskos sa may dapog. Buminuhat siya sa banig para imodon ini. Sayo na daco na ayam an inabutan niya. Inatubang siya sang ayam asin gin parabahu-baho siya. Ang inisip niya basi nagugutom ang ayam kaya binahug niya. Diri mang nagkaon ang ayam kundi lalo ini nagdarag ni kaniya. Nahadok na si Pay Blas. Diri ini ordinaryo na ayam ang saisip niya. Lalo siya nahadok sang luksuhan siya san ayam mayad ngani nakadulag siya.

---

[43] Contributed by Shirley F. Vera, from Bulan, Sorsogon, who had it from Ernesto Gisala, from the same town, who in turn heard it from Blas Baculong, a high school graduate.

Ang hinimo niya halbuton ang sundang nang tinigbas ang
ayam. Pagkatapos lalo nagkurulogon ang kaniya lawas kaya
hinulog lang niya ang mamamatayon na ayam sa luwas. San
magabihon, diri siya makaturog kay baga sin ginyuyogyog
ang kaniya balay. Sa bubong, may nag-uuntol na mga bato.
Nag-dong lang ini san pagturaok san mga manok. Ki-
naagahan, nag-uli siya sa kaniya familya sa Iraga kay may
suspetsa siya na ang asuwang na yadto ay ang kanira katang-
ing na si Dalmacio.

   Inabutan niya ang asawa ni Dalmacio nagsisilhig kan
kanira natad. Hinapot niya kung nain si Dalmacio. Sabi man
san babaye mahapdos kay nagkarigos kanina na alas kuatro sa
dagat nang pag-uli gin paragulan sa lawas. Nag-ayo siya sin
permiso na makaistorya si Dalmacio pero habo nagtugot an
babaye. Sumakat na lang diretso sa balay si Blas nang inabu-
tan niya si Dalmacio naturog sa katre. Nahali na lang siya
sang maimod niya ang palanggana na puno sin dugo, sa may
sirong san katre. Rumani si Pay Blas nang isabihan ang
nakataklop na tanong sa lawas sini. Naimod niya na puro
dugo. Yinugyog niya si Dalmacio nang sinabi sa "Padre, diri
kamagbuwa. Ikaw pa lang ang nag-asuwang saaco kagab-i."
Pagkatapos lumuwas na siya sa balay. Diri pa ngani siya
nakaharag-yo, may nagngurunguyan na. Idto palan, kay si
Dalmacio namatay na.

Uncle Blas lived alone in a small hut on his clearing
in Pon-od. He had a particular illness which usually attacked in the late afternoon and throughout the evening.
He constantly quivered with cold or lost his energy. One
night, his illness weakened him again so he was not able
to eat his evening meal. After tightly bolting the single
door and two windows of his hut, he fixed his bed and
lay down to sleep. When he was about to close his eyes,
he heard a noise in the little kitchen. He got up and
went to see what it was. It was only a big dog, he
thought. The animal faced him and started sniffing him.
Thinking that the dog was hungry, he brought out his
food and fed the large animal. But it refused to eat; in-

stead, it attacked him. By fast action, he dodged the dog. With a quick movement, he grabbed the sharp bolo from the wall and struck the dog. The pain in his body had already weakened him so that he just kicked the writhing dog outside. It was already past twelve when the hut started shaking and big stones rained on the roof. This stopped only when the roosters started crowing. The next morning he decided to go to his family in Iraga with a suspicion that the aswang was Dalmacio, their neighbor.

Dalmacio's wife was sweeping the yard as he passed by. He inquired about Dalmacio's whereabouts and the woman told him that her husband was ill after having had a swim in the sea. Uncle Blas asked permission to visit him but the old woman angrily refused. He ignored the woman's attitude and barged into the house where he found Dalmacio in bed. He was in a deep sleep. Uncle Blas was about to leave when he noticed a small basin under a bed. It was half full of blood dripping from the wooden bed. He approached Dalmacio and abruptly pulled the blanket from his body. Blood smeared the whole bed. He was shocked and terrified. Dalmacio, upon seeing him, attempted to get up but he could not. Uncle Blas, red-faced with anger, angrily accused Dalmacio of pestering him and threatened to kill him if he should do it again. Dalmacio did not say anything. After this short confrontation Uncle Blas rapidly left the house with anger still on his face. Only a short distance away, he heard Damacio's wife wailing. Uncle Blas understood that Dalmacio had died.

19. [WEREDOG AT A CHILDBIRTH][44]

In one of the towns of Samar known as Paranas, a horrifying incident happened. It took place in a small hut owned by a couple. The wife was about to give birth to her first child. Her husband left in order to fetch the midwife, leaving his wife alone. While he was away, an old woman with long, ungroomed hair, sharp eyes, and long nails entered the house.

Upon entering the room, she approached the woman at labor inside the mosquito net. The intrusion shocked the woman and she fainted.

Luckily, her husband and the midwife arrived in time and saw the horrible appearance of an old woman who was about to harm the woman at labor. Upon knowing their presence, the old woman tried to escape through the window. The husband ran after her with his bolo. After a chase he witnessed the change in appearance of the old woman into a big pig with her wooden clogs still on. Then the pig was lost in the darkness. Later he came to know through his wife that the aswang was no other than their neighbor Kikay.

The following day, the incident became the talk of the town, and this made the townspeople fear the presence of the old woman. Their fear was strengthened by their having often seen her walking alone in the dark night.

---

[44] Contibuted by Iniceta Soriano, from San Miguel, Bulacan, who had it in English from Dora B. Chicano, from Paranas, Western Samar.

20. [A WEREDOG HUSBAND][45]
Waray Text

Hadto nga panahon han nga Kastila, may ada mag-asawa nga gin ngaranan kan Ruben ngan hi Angelita. Damo an nasiring nga an pamilia nira Ruben gin tatahapa nga aswang.

Osa pala kabolan hira nga ikinasal. Osa hadto ka gab-i nga bolanon nagsarit hi Ruben han iya asawa nga mamamasyada daw kono hiya diri la maiha kay inaalinsooban hiya. Naglabay in pira ka oras waray sabot hi Angelita nga inabot hi Ruben.

Pagkabowas la naestoryahan hira nga may ada pinatay nga tawo didto han ligid han buybayon nga dako an kasamdan dida han liog nga pariho hin tinokob hin ayam. Pira la ka beses nga nanarit hi Ruben kan Angelita nga mamamasyada. Kada paggigikan niya han balay may nakaestorya nga may natapo nga patay dida han aga. Gin bowaan la nga gin tatahapan ni Angelita an iya asawa nga diri niya totooron an mga somatsomat tongod han iya asawa iya gin senonod adto nga sarit ha iya. Sinonod niya hi Ruben ngan nakita niya nga nagserong han ira balay didto han tabok han kwarto han iya nanong nga maysakit nga TB. Pagatokang niya han kwarto han iya namang, nakita niya nga an iya asawa nga nanamamarahibo hin itom ngan pinanodkan hin tango. Nahimo hiya nga maitom nga ayam nga nan momolagdat ang mga mata. Guinmoliat hi Angelita ngan nagkadaop an ira aramyaw nga may ada mga dara nga sondang ngan hin ibaralbag. Ginbaralbag nira an dako nga ayam ngada han kamatay. Ginmangnoan nira ngada han pagsidlit han adlaw. Nakita nira nga nagbabag-o an klase han ayam yan ngan nahimo nga tawo waray iba hon deri hi Ruben.

[45] Contributed by Anita E. Estonilo, from Lilio, Laguna, who had it from Naty Olfendo, a former housemaid from Olaog, Basey, Samar, who in turn heard it from Pising Pacaanas, from the same locality.

In the times of the Castilians [Spaniards] there was a couple, Ruben and Angelita. Some said that the family of Ruben were aswang.

They had been married only a month when one night when the moon was perfectly round, Ruben asked the permission of his wife to go out to take a walk because he was feeling warm. Angelita did not know what time Ruben came back because she was asleep then.

Next morning there was news that a man had been killed near the river. This man had a bite in his neck like that of a dog. Every time Ruben went out there was a murder. So Angelita suspected him. One night when Ruben went out again, his wife followed him. Angelita saw that Ruben went under their house, near her aunt's room. Actually, her aunt was sick with tuberculosis. When Ruben was near the room of Angelita's aunt, Angelita saw that black hair was growing over the whole body of Ruben and then he was changed into a big black dog. Upon seeing him, she screamed very loud and the neighbors were all awakened and came over. The neighbors brought bolos and pieces of wood and anything that they could use to beat the dog. The dog was killed. They waited for the morning and the dog changed to its original appearance as a man. The dog was none other than Ruben.

21. [PIG LICKING PATIENT'S BODY][46]

I was only twelve years old when I heard this story from one of our maids in Samar.

There was a sick man of about forty in Oras, Samar. He was living with his married son. Their house was very small and the floor very low. The old man had been ill for many months. He was very thin.

One night while his son was looking out of the win-

---

[46] Contributed by Evelyn Lorenzo, from Mexico, Pampanga, who heard it in English from Orlando Solidon, from Borongan, Samar.

dow, he saw a winged person flying who turned into a very big pig on touching the ground. The son could not tell whether it was a man or a woman. From the yard the pig went under the house.

The son took his bolo and went out. He saw the pig extending its tongue and licking the body of his sleeping father. Their floor was made of bamboo, and at the sight he thrust his bolo into the body of the pig.

The pig was wounded but it ran away, changing its form into that of a person with wings as it flew away.

The son decided to consult a *manghuhula* (fortune teller). The family learned from him that the aswang came from the Bicol region. The manghuhula gave instructions to the son. He said the manghuhula had gone to Bicol.

When they found the house of the aswang, the son buried a raw chicken egg under the ladder. Then he entered the house, passing through the kitchen. He lighted a cigarette he had brought for the purpose. He saw a man with a wound being treated by an old woman. She placed a coconut shell over the fire and when it was moist she applied this to the wound. After that the son went out and threw the lighted cigarette on the spot where the egg was buried. They just then heard the old woman crying, saying that her son was dead.

22. [A DOG SENT HOME][47]
Tagalog Text

Noong araw, nang dalaga pa si Nana Goniang, umigib siya ng tubig sa poso na nasa liwasang bayan pa. Gabi na noon. Nang nasa may poso na siya, nakakita siya ng isang malaking aso. Hindi siya natakot sapagkat kilala niya iyon. Nang malapit na siya sa aso, sinabi niya, "Tura, gabi na.

---

[47] Contributed by Hermelina M. Villarosa, of Rosario, Cavite, who heard it from Trinidad Mercado, of Catarman, Samar.

Umuwi ka na." Pagkasabi niyon, iyon ay nagpalit ng anyo at naging baboy at umuwi.

When Nana Goniang was still a young lady, she fetched water from the artesian well which was still at the town plaza. It was late in the evening. When she was at the artesian well, she saw a big dog. She did not fear it because she knew it. When she was near the dog, she said, "Tura, it's getting late. You go home now." It changed its appearance and became a pig and went home.

23. [ASWANG VOMITS OBJECTS AT HIS DEATH][48]
Tagalog Text

Sa aming bayan ay may tao na ang pangalan ay Mang Tura. Si Mang Tura ay nag-iiba ng anyo kung gabi. Siya ay nagiging malaking aso, baboy, o pusa. Dahil nga sa siya ay isang aswang, noong siya ay malapit nang mamatay ay may iniluwa siyang isang bagay na kulay berde.

In our town there was a man named Mang Tura. Mang Tura's appearance changed at night. He became a big dog, pig, or cat. Because he was an aswang, when he was about to die he vomited a certain thing colored green.

---

[48] Contributed by Hermelina M. Villarosa, of Rosario, Cavite, who heard it in Tagalog from Trinidad Mercado, of Catarman, Samar.

24. [PIG UNDER PATIENT'S BED][49]
Tagalog Text

Ang kuwentong ito ng aking lola ay matagal nang nang-yari. Mayroon daw isang pamilya sa aming nayon na may matandang babaeng nagkasakit nang malubha. Hindi nila ma-laman kung ano ang dahilan ng sakit at ayaw gumaling. Noon daw magkasakit ang babae ay may nagpuntang baboy na itim sa silong ng bahay at ayaw raw umalis. Sisilip-silip lamang sa sahig ng bahay. Mahaba ang nguso at lumalapad ang tainga. Ang ginawa nila ay nagsunog ng sungay ng kala-baw at ipinaamoy sa baboy. Umalis ang baboy at noon pa la-mang gumaling na ang babae.

This story from my grandmother happened long ago. There was a family in our village whose old-woman member became seriously ill. They did not know what caused her illness or why she did not get well. It is said that when she got sick, a black hog went under her house and did not want to leave. The hog would just occasionally peep through the flooring of the house. He had a long snout and his ears would become wider and wider. The family burned the horns of a carabao and let the hog smell the smoke. The hog left and only then did the woman get well.

[49] Contributed by Immaculada B. Blancaflor, from Santa, Ilocos Sur, who had it from Leonie Alvisa, a former housemaid from Kapuukan, Leyte.

25. [THE WEREDOG THAT FOUGHT A DOG][50]
Waray Text

*Si Toyang ngan si Enting mag-asawa. Si Toyang hinga-
rak-an. Si Enting may sakit sin danlak. Nang kon atakihan
siya, dayon la niya pag-kinaskasan sit iya sista. May-ada nira
etoy. An ira balay, sa daplin sin daliri nga hinimo sin nipa,
guintakilan sin taklap an purta.*

*Usa ka gab-i guin-ataki si Enting san iya danlak. Guin-
kuha dayon an iya sista, pero pagtindog niya, nakakita siya
sin mga maingat nga mga mata sa purta. Guin-abot siya sin
kakulba. Iya guin sangpit si Toyang pero binsa gud niya an-
hon pag-ug-og, waray gid makamata. Hasta nga guinapasan
si Enting sin aswang. An etoy nira nga hapit na unta niya
pataya, amo an nakasalbar kan Enting. Guin paangan leog
ngan guinkamras ang mga mata san aswang hasta nga
nahulog ini sa pangpang ngan namatay. Si Enting guin-
pusdak sa lunayan. Waray baya'i san etoy si Enting hasta san
kaaga.*

Toyang and Enting were a married couple. Toyang
was pregnant. Enting had *danlak,* a sickness whereby his
testicles grew big. Whenever he had an attack he would
just keep on tuning his guitar. They had a little dog.
Their house was near a river and was made of nipa
thatch, and their door was covered with a blanket.

One night Enting had an attack. He rose to get his
guitar but when he got up, he saw two big bright eyes
near the door. He was beginning to fear. He tried to
wake Toyang up, but no matter how much he shook
her, she didn't wake up. Enting was carried off by the
aswang. A little dog which they had nearly killed saved
Enting. It bit the aswang's neck and tore its eyes out,
too, until it fell down from a cliff and died. Enting was
thrown into a muddy canal. The dog did not leave
Enting till dawn.

---

[50] Contributed by Wenceslao Kantindoy, Jr., from Abuyog, Leyte, who
had it from Eufemia Barcelon, from Hampipila, Abuyog.

26. [THE CREATURE OF CHANGING SHAPES][51]
Waray Text

Si Demy ngan si Bayong nga burod, naningba san maagahon, mga alas-kuwatro san kaagahan. Desembre—mahagkot. San tiharani na sira san bulangan, nakakita sira sin uding. Waray la anay ini nira igkabali. Pero san nahimo an uding nga ayam, guin-abot sira sin kahadlok; katima, nahimo na liwat ini nga ayam ngadto sa baboy. Nahingdok sira nakadali. An baboy nagsinunga. Katima la, paghitungod nira san bulangan, ini nga baboy nahimo ngadto san tawo nga ora-ora sin kaniwang. Nangiyak sira nga duha, nanalagan, nga waray makapaningba.

Demy and Bayong, who was pregnant, went to mass early in the morning about four o'clock. December-cold. When they were nearing the cockpit house, they saw a cat. They didn't mind it. But when the cat changed into a dog, fear came into their hearts; then this dog changed into a pig. They were for a moment motionless. The pig was groaning. Afterward when they were by the cockpit house, the pig changed into a very thin man. They cried for help, ran, and failed to hear mass.

27. [AN ASWANG SPEARED][52]

It was night when the uncle of Endoy was suffering from a stomachache. Tata, Endoy's uncle, was bending and bowing and was making a lot of noise because of pain. There was a hole in one of the corners of the house where he was spitting. He vomited a yellowish

---

[51] Contributed by Wenceslao R. Katindoy, Jr., from Abuyog, Leyte, who had it from Enrico Katindoy, from the same town.

[52] Contributed by Aurora A. Brazal, who had it in English from Wenceslao Katindoy, then a college student from Abuyog, Leyte.

liquid. Even though he was in pain, he sensed that there was someone under the house. He heard a grunting sound and a pounding on the ground. So he slowly crawled to get his spear and then thrust it into the hole where he was spitting.

Next morning there was news that one of his neighbors was dead with a wound in his neck. Tata was afraid but he didn't tell what happened the previous night. He suspected right away that that man was the one under his house.

28. [THE BLACK CAT][53]
Tagalog Text

Nangyari raw ang kuwentong ito noong 1936 sa aming bahay sa Tijiron, Makati, Rizal. Kasalukuyan daw nagdadalantao ang aking ina sa aking Kuya Peling. Tuwing gabi raw ay may isang malaking pusang itim na ligid nang ligid sa aming bahay. Noong una raw ay hindi ito pansin ng aking lola, pero nang may ilang gabi na ang nagdaan at malapit nang manganak ang aking nanay ay natakot na ang aking lola kaya sinabi niya sa aking itay ang tungkol sa malaking pusang itim. Nang tingnan ng Itay ang pusa ay nakita raw niya na ito ay napakalaki at bigla raw umakyat sa aming bubungan at ito raw ay nawala. Kaya ang kanila raw ginawa ay kumuha sila ng maraming bawang at abo at nang sumunod raw na gabi ang mga bawang at abo ay kanilang ikinalat sa buong bahay. Mula raw nuon ang malaking pusa ay hindi na bumalik sa aming tahanan.

It is said that this story happened in our house in Tijiron, Makati, Rizal, in 1936. My mother was said to be heavy with my eldest brother Peling. Every night there was a large black cat circling our house. At first my

---

[53] Contributed by Feliciana B. Parrilla, from Tuburan, Cebu, who had it from Prima Rivera, from Taguig, Rizal.

grandmother did not pay attention to this, but after a few nights, when my mother was about to give birth, my grandmother was worried and so she told my father about the big black cat. When my father investigated, he saw the cat and it suddenly climbed to the rooftop and disappeared. So what they did was to get lots of garlic and ashes and the following night they scattered the garlic and ashes all over the house. After that the big cat did not come back to our house.

29. [A BOUT WITH AN ASWANG][54]
Kiniray-a Text

Dia ang bantog nga istorya sa amon banwa. Katong 1960 ginbaya-an ni Juan ang anang asawa kag bata para magbakal sang sigarilyo sa ilawod. Mga alas nueve sa gab-i nag-abot ang aswang sa balay ni Juan kag guindomog ang anang asawa. Ang tuyo sang aswang amo ang darwa ka tu-ig nga bata. Nagbato ang asawa na pero madanlog ang lawas cang aswang.

Ginkagat na ang tudlo kang aswang kundi nagpalagyo. Ginsugid na kay Juan ang natabu. Sunod nga mga adlaw nagpahimos si Juan sang isa ka ponsyon. Gin-imbitar ni Juan ang suspetsado nga aswang sa compleaño sang bata na. Masadya ang lawas sang aswang pero indi na naman-an nga ang mga pagka-on kontra cana. Nagbarahul ang mga mata cang aswang cang nakita na ang pagka-on nga duro asin hay sayod kananda nga mga aswang. Mapalagyo ra-ad pero gin taya-an ni Juan cang pusil kag ginkun-an na nga maghalin sa banwa kay kon indi patyen na tana.

This is a story that spread throughout my town. In 1960 Juan left his wife and his child to buy some cigarettes in the town. It was around 9 PM when an aswang

---

[54] Contributed by Regino V. Hofileña, from San Jose, Antique, who had it from Juan Santa Maria, a government employee from the same town.

came and wrestled with Juan's wife. The objective of the aswang was the two-year-old child of Juan. Juan's wife fought back but could not take hold of its oily body.

Then she bit the thumb of the aswang and the aswang went away. She reported the incident to her husband and a few days later Juan prepared a good luncheon. Juan invited the suspected aswang to eat with them, for it was his child's birthday. The aswang was happy that she could carry out her plans but didn't know that Juan had prepared food harmful to the aswang. When the aswang sat at the table, her eyes grew big on seeing the food with spices and salt. She tried to get away, but Juan drew his rifle and told the aswang to get out of the town or be killed.

30. [TO FIGHT AN ASWANG][55]
Kiniray-a Text

Ang mananggiti nga si Minyong nga naga-istar sa ingod can baybay sang amon banwa ang nag-istorya canakon cadia.

Nanaog tana sa ana balay cang a las nueve sang gabi-i para magpamos-on. Nakauba lang cang pantalon na cag makita na ang tao nga nagatuwad. Dayon an be-el cang sanggot na, cag dumog na ang aswang. Madanlog ang lawas cang aswang cag si Minyong hindi makakaput cana. Ginuyod can aswang paagto sa dagat pero ginkagat ni Minyong ang tudlona. Nabuy-an tana ang aswang. Na-abot ni Minyong ang sanggotna kag binunona ang aswang . Naglupad ang aswang nga naga huni nga "Ik-ik-ik". Pagkasunod nga aga, may hambal nga may tao nga nahulog sa niyog sa pihak ka baryo kag ang may kutsilyo nga naka-igo sa anang lawas. Ginagtonan ni Minyong ang tao kag ginsugidanon. Nakilala

[55] Contributed by Regino V. Hofileña, from San Jose, Antique, who had it from Herminio Pacune, a tuba gatherer from the same town.

na ang tao nga manogbaligya cang tuba. Pagpanaog ni
Minyong ginbaliskad na cang andang hagdan. Tudi pa
marayo si Minyong kag mabugto cang ginhawa can aswang.
Ang pagsulang ni Minyong cang aswang amo ang nagpatay
kana.

✑

A tuba gatherer, Minyong, living on the seacoast of
our town, told me this story.

He left his house about 9 PM to move his bowels. He
had just removed his pants when he saw a man standing with head down and staring at him. Before he could
reach for his half-moon knife, the man, an aswang,
wrestled with him. The aswang's body was oily so that
Minyong could not grasp a single part of it. The aswang
tried to drag Minyong into the water, but Minyong bit
his thumb and was able to get away. Minyong reached
for his half-moon knife and stabbed the aswang. The
aswang flew in pain and cried, "Ik-ik-ik." Morning came
and news spread that someone fell from a coconut tree
in a nearby barrio and his knife hit him. Minyong went
to see this man, it was his rival at selling tuba (coconut
sap wine). Minyong talked with him and as Minyong
left he put the stairs upside down. Minyong had gone
just a yard when the man died.

31. [WEREDOG IN AKLAN][56]
Tagalog Text

Noong panahon din ng Hapon si Tay Itik—kasi gerilya
siya kasama nila Tio Nonoy—inutusan siya magdeliver ng
message sa Tio Nonoy. Inabot siya ng gabi kaya nakitulog
siya sa isang bahay na may mag-asawang matanda. Noong
gabi na nilagay niya 'yung carbine na dala niya sa tabi niya.
Tapos noong medyo alas dose napansin niya na may apoy sa

---

[56] Contributed by Edelmira T. Manikan, who had it in Tagalog from
Orlando G. Orencio, a high school sophomore from Unat, Ibajay, Aklan.

kusina. Tapos pumasok 'yung matandang lalaki sa kuarto na may dalang kutsilyo—papalapit sa kaniya. Pinaputuk niya ang carbine—tapos ginising siya ng matanda, pero gising na siya. Tinanong kung ano ang nangyari sa kaniya. Sinabi niya nanaginip lang siya. Tapos nagpaalam na siya at umalis.

❧

During the Japanese times also, Tay Itik—because he was a guerrilla with Tio Nonoy—was sent to deliver a message to Tio Nonoy. Night caught up with him and so he sought shelter in the house of an old couple. When it was time for them to sleep, he placed the carbine he had brought with him at his side. When it was near twelve o'clock he noticed that there was fire in the kitchen. After that the old man came into the room with a knife in his hand, approaching him. He fired the carbine—then the old man woke him up, but he was already awake. He was asked what had happened to him, and he told the old man he was just dreaming. Then he said goodbye and left.

32. [THE *KOROKOTO*][57]
Cebu-Visayan Text

Kung mulakaw ang koroko, ang iyang tiil wala niya sabda ang yuta. Gatago siya sa mga kahoy ug sagbot. Makahimo siya ug porma sa iro ug iring. Madumog niya ang iyang mga biktima, ginadala niya sa balay, ginaluto ug kinakaon. Mahibaw-an siya sa iyang tingog nga "Kotokoto."

Usa ka gabii, sa kagubatan nga utlanan sa Davao ug Cotabato, may mga PC nga gisugo nga pangitaon sa mga kolono nga nakabuhi ug nagtago diha. Ang usa ka PC nga nahilayo sa iyang mga kauban, nakakita ug tawo sa unahan. Nangutana ang sundalo kon kinsa ang tawo. Murag nagtubag

---

[57] Contributed by Kenneth Edward Lim, from Davao City, recalling an incident during his past association with Davao peasants.

ang tawo, galing kay dili kaayo madunggan. Pero pag duol sa tawo na hibapan sa sundalo nga ang tawo wala nagtubag sa iyang pangutana. Ang tawo, naghimo ug tingog nga murag "Koro-koto." Natingala ang PC kay ang paglakaw sa tawo wala nga iro. Nahadlok ang PC nga sundalo ug nagdagan siya nga kusug nagasangga sa yuta iyang tiil—naa lang sa hangin. Gitudlo sa sundalo ang iyang pusil sa aswang apan ang korokoto nahimo ng itom kaayo. Pagkaadlaw, nakita siya dose kilometros sa iya nagikanan. Ingon nila nga ang "adrenalin" niya tingalo ang rason (sa iyang pagdagan ug layo sa pila lang ka oras).

⌒

When the *korokoto* walks, his feet do not touch the ground. He seeks shelter in trees and bushes. He can take the form of a dog or a cat. He wrestles with his victims, drags them home, cooks them, and eats them. He can be identified by the sound he emits—"Koro-koto."

One night, in the forest at the boundary line between Davao and Cotabato, Philippine Constabulary men were ordered to spread out and comb the area for escaped convicts believed to have sought refuge there. A PC ranger who had been separated from his companions espied a man before him. The ranger asked the man to identify himself. The man seemed to give a muffled reply. But as the stranger drew nearer, the soldier realized that he was not responding to his request. The man was murmuring something which sounded like "Koro-koto." To the PC ranger's discomposure, the man was not treading the earth—he was walking on air. When the trained combatant aimed his rifle at the creature, the *korokoto* quickly assumed the form of a black dog. The ranger was frightened, and he ran as fast as he could.

The next day the PC trooper found that he had run 12 kilometers without his knowledge. It was theorized that his adrenalin was responsible for this phenomenon (of his having covered the distance in a few hours.)

33. [A BASILAN ASWANG][58]
Tagalog Text

Sa amin sa Sulu, ang mga tao ay hindi masyadong nani-niwala sa aswang, pero may kaibigan akong taga-Basilan, Zamboanga del Sur, na may bida tungkol dito. Ang paniwala nila, ang mga aswang daw ay nakikilala dahil sa mapupula nilang mata at sila daw ay nakatira sa gubat. Malalaman mo kung may papatayin ang aswang sapagkat biglang nagiging pulang-pula ang kanyang mga mata. Karaniwang pinapatay nila ay yuong mga taong naglalakad mag-isa.

Isang kababayan daw niya ang naglalakad na mag-isa gal-ing sa isang kasayahan, ang naging biktima ng aswang. Sa paglalakad niya ay nasalubong ito ng isang tao na tumitig sa kanya nang malalim. Para siyang sumunod na lang dito na parang hindi nalalaman ang kaniyang ginagawa. Ang tao ay nawawala ngunit ito ay nakasunod pa sa kanya. Hindi niya ito nakikita, pero nakikita siya nito. Pinakakain pa siya ng aswang ng mga pagkaing hindi pangkaraniwan, katulad ng sariwang ahas, bulati, at sari-saring mga damo. Maraming mga kababayan ay nagtulong-tulong ng paghahanap sa kaniya ngunit inabot na sila ng isang buwan ay hindi pa nila ito nakikita. Nawalan na sila ng interes at binayaan na lamang ito sa kaniyang pagkawala.

Pagkalipas ng dalawang buwan ay bigla na lamang lumi-taw ang nawawalang tao. Ngunit iba na ang kilos niya. Matalim siyang tumingin at tila naloloko. Isang gabi ay nakita ng isang kapit-bahay na siya ay aali-aligid sa bahay ng isang maysakit at tila may inaamoy. Kinabukasan ay namatay ang maysakit doon. Isinumbong naman ng kapitbahay sa ama ng namatay ang nakita niya noong isang gabi. Ang ama ng namatay ay naghuramentado at sumugod sa bahay nina Mo-hammad, yung taong nakuha na aswang, at siya pinatay. Pagkatapos ay nagpakamatay din ang ama ng namatay.

---

[58] Contributed by Vivian B. Manalo, of Pasig, Rizal, who had it in Tagalog from Isiah Adiong, of Sulu.

In our place in Sulu, people do not believe much in aswang, but I have a friend from Basilan, Zamboanga del Sur, who has a story about this. Their belief is that the aswang can be distinguished because their eyes are red and they live in the forest. You will know when the aswang will kill because their eyes suddenly become very, very red. They usually attack people caught walking alone.

He said a man from his hometown was walking alone after he had been to a party one night and was the victim of the aswang. He met a person in his walk who stared at him sharply. He followed him blindly and seemed not to know what he was doing. The person who stared at him was lost from sight but was still following him. He did not see the man but the man saw him. He was fed with peculiar food like raw snakes, worms, and various kinds of grass. Many of his neighbors helped each other in looking for him, but a month passed and he was not yet seen. They lost interest and just let him remain lost whatever might happen to him.

After two months, the lost boy suddenly showed up. But his actions were a lot different. He looked sharply at people and seemed to be insane. One night a neighbor saw him loitering around a house where someone was ill and he seemed to be smelling something. The next day the sick person there was dead. The neighbor told the father what he had seen that night. The father of the dead one ran amok, advanced to the house of Mohammed, the one taken by the aswang, and killed him. Then the father committed suicide.

Viscera Sucker Legends

34. [A VISCERA-TAKING WIFE][59]

Almost immediately after the couple had moved to Narvacan, Ilocos Sur, the neighbors noticed that the woman was very unneighborly. She almost never went out by day but she would usually be seen arriving home in the wee·hours of the morning.

One night, at 1:30, a neighbor went out to the river bank for necessity but never came back. At 3:00 AM the wife found him by the bank of the river, his abdomen open and the insides gone. Naturally they suspected the new neighbors, and the husband came to know of it.

The husband got suspicious too, and so he asked the wife where she was getting all the intestines they were always having for viand. She replied that she bought them from a friend. The husband did not believe her story, so he began to observe his wife's activities. Then one night he found the lower body of his wife hidden behind the kitchen door, and with a heavy heart he sprinkled ashes on it. At about 4:00 AM, the upper body

---

[59] Contributed by Aida B. Ayong, from Ifugao Province, who had it in English from Daisy Ontiveros, a teacher from Aparri, Cagayan, and who in turn heard it from Trinidad Umandap, from Narvacan, Ilocos Sur.

of the wife came home but could not connect with her - lower body, so it cried and begged forgiveness from the husband but nothing else could be done. She then placed her upper part to sit on her lower part and died.

35. [PROTECTION FOR A WOMAN
IN CHILDBIRTH][60]
Iloko Text

Idiay ili tayo a San Narciso, Zambales, dagiti lallakay ken babbaket dida baybay-an a maturog ti naganak. Kunada a no dandani aganak ti masicogen, ti aswang a kasla billet ket ag-taytayab iti ngato ti balay ti aganak, kunana, "Ik-ik-ik!" In-tono kuan, agbalin a babae sa sumiroc iti balay sa sepsepenna ti dara nga agwayaway iti naganak. Ti naganak masapul a saan a pulos a maturog ti agpatpatnag, ta no makaturog ket sida ti aswang ti ubing. Dagiti tao mangipanda iti bawang iti pasamano ti tawa, agpuorda iti sibay ti tawa, agpuorda iti sibay ti masicog, sada agpuor iti nasallapid a daan a luplupot.

In our town of San Narciso, Zambales, the old folks do not permit a pregnant woman to sleep when she gives birth. They say that when she is about to give birth the aswang in the form of a bird flies over the house and says, "Ik-ik-ik." Then it changes into a woman and it goes under the house and sips the blood that flows out of the mother. The mother has to remain wide awake throughout the night or else the aswang will eat the baby. To keep away the aswang, people put garlic on the window sill, and they build a small fire near the window and near the pregnant woman and burn braided old clothes.

---

[60] Contributed by Aurora A. Brazal, of San Narciso, Zambales, who had it from Leonor A. Brazal, a supervising nurse in the same town.

36. [THE SEWING THREAD][61]
Tagalog Text

May paniniwala sa aming bayan ng Morong, Bataan, na masama sa isang buntis ang manahi ng damit. Nguni't isang gabi, isang buntis ang nagsusulsi ng damit. Habang hinahatak niya ang sinulid, napansin niya na ito'y napakahaba kaya kinuha niya ang gunting at ginupit niya ito. Narinig niya na may bumagsak at dumaing sa lupa sa ilalim ng bahay. Bumaba siya upang magsiyasat. May nakita siyang ibon na naghihingalo. Siya'y naniwala na aswang ang ibong yaon.

There is a belief in our town, Morong, Bataan, that it is bad for a pregnant woman to sew clothes.[62] But one night a pregnant woman was darning clothes. While pulling the thread, she noticed that it was too long, so she got her scissors and snipped it. She heard a thud on the ground under the house and then there was a groan. She went to investigate, and she saw a bird in the throes of death. She believed that the bird was an aswang.

37. [THE *TIKTIK* IN NOVALICHES][63]

When I was pregnant with your brother Spanky in Bagbag, Novaliches, there was, every night, a *tiktik* hovering over our place. It was very noisy and nobody could sleep. After the tiktik, someone seemed to be scratching the wall and the sound also was as if a big animal was roaming around the area.

---

[61] Contributed by Aurora A. Brazal, of San Narciso, Zambales, who had it from Elvira Dizon, from Morong, Bataan.

[62] The belief among the Iloko of Zambales is that at birth the baby of a mother who sewed clothes during her pregnancy will be strangeld by its umbilical cord.

[63] Contributed by Edelmira T. Manikan, who had it in English from her mother, a pharmacist.

So what your uncles did was to bring a *buntot-pagi* (ray's tail) and bolo and they went out of the house. And they saw this big pig and they ran after it, but they did not catch up with it. Then they saw this fellow hiding behind one of the ruined pillars.

The next night, I was bothered by the tiktik again and when I looked out of the window, I saw a big cat, one as big as a *biik* (little pig). So your uncles approached this fellow and they ran after the pig and warned it that if anything happened to me, they would kill it. After that the disturbance did not happen again.

We were not the only ones who suffered from these disturbances. Even the neighbors couldn't get to sleep.

38. [THE TAXI DANCER][64]
Tagalog Text

Noon, matagal na, sa aming bayan ay mayroon kaming kabaret o salon—iyon bang sayawan ng mga belyas. Maraming belyas na nakatira sa isa naming bahay. Kung taga-tagasaan. Mayroong taga-Bicol at taga-Bisaya. May kanya-kanya silang kuwarto. Sila ay nagsasayaw sa gabi at natutulog sa araw, parang mga kuwago. Ang isang sayaw sa kanila ay diyes sentimos.

May isa kaming belyas na taga-Bisaya, at napupuna namin na sa tuwing sasapit ang alas-onse y medya ng gabi na kabilugan ang buwan ay umaalis siya sa kabaret kahit na siya ay may kasayaw. Siya ay pumupunta sa kanyang kuwarto at ikakandado niya ang pintuan. Siya ay babalik ng mga alas-dos na ng madaling araw sa kabaret at magsasayaw na muli.

Ito ay lagi kong napapansin at isang gabi ay sinundan ko siya at nakita kong pumasok siya sa kanyang silid at ikinandado ang pintuan. Ang ginawa ko ay naghanap ako ng butas

[64] Contributed by Anita E. Estonilo, from Lilio, Laguna, who had it from Eduardo Borlaza, a high school graduate from the same town.

na masisilipan at nakita ko siya na may ipinapahid sa kan-
yang katawan at nag-iiba ang kanyang mukha. Pagkatapos
unti-unting natatanggal ang kalahati ng kanyang katawan sa
may baywang at saka ang lansa ng amoy. Nakita kong nag-
lilibot ang itaas ng kalahati ng kanyang katawan sa kanyang
kuwarto. Tumakbo ako dahil sa takot. Kinabukasan ay ibinali-
ta ko sa tiyo ko ang nakita ko at siya ay pinaalis na. Malan-
sang malansa ang amoy ng kanyang silid.

～

Once, a long time since, we had a cabaret—you
know, a dancing place for taxi-dancers—in our town.
There were many dancers living in one of the houses in
town. They were from different places. Some of them
were from the Bicol area and others were from the
Visayan islands. Each had her own room. They danced
at night and slept by day, like the owls. One dance with
them cost ten centavos.

We had one Visayan dancer, and we noticed that
whenever eleven-thirty struck when the moon was at its
full, she would go out or leave her partner to go to her
room and lock her door. Then at two o'clock she would
come back to the cabaret and dance again.

I always noticed this and one night I followed her
and saw that she went inside her room and locked the
door. I found a hole through which I could peep and
through the hole I saw her rubbing something on her
body and her face was changing. Then her body was
slowly separated at the waist—and how fishy the smell!
I saw that her upper body was circling inside her room.
I ran in terror. The next day I told this to my uncle and
he let her go. The smell of her room was very fishy.

39. [THE ASWANG DELEGATION][65]
Tagalog Text

Noong taong 1930 isang seminar ng mga guro ang idinaos sa Lucban, Quezon. Ang lahat ng bayan sa lalawigan ng Quezon ay nagpadala ng mga delegado. Ang mga ito ay itinira sa mga gusali ng mababang paaralan, isang kilometro ang layo mula sa kabayanan. Ang seminar ay tumagal ng isang linggo. Noong gabi pagkatapos na magdatingan ang mga delegado, ang mga taong naninirahan malapit sa bakuran ng paaralan ay nakarinig ng kakaibang ingay ng mga lumilipad na pakpak at ang huni na "tik-tik-tik" ng ibong tiktik. Matibay ang paniniwala ng bayang ito na kapag narinig ang huni ng tiktik sa gabi ay mayroong aswang o mga aswang sa paligid.

Nang sumunod na gabi, ang ilan sa mga taong may malakas na loob ay sumilip mula sa mga bintana nang may marinig na parang lumilipad. Gayon na lamang ang takot nila ng makita ang isang kawan ng mga nilalang na may maiitim na pakpak na lumilipad sa kadiliman ng gabi. Ang mga ito ay may ulo at katawan ng tao nguni't putol ang katawan mula sa baywang hanggang ibaba. Naghinala ang mga tao na ang nakita nila ay mga manananggal.

Kinabukasan, ang mga taga-Lucban na nag-asikaso sa pagpapakain sa mga delegado ay nagmasid na mabuti sa mga ito. Napansin nila na ang ilan sa mga delegado ay ayaw kumain ng mga pagkaing maraming rekado at ang gustong-gusto ay dinuguan at inihaw na lamang loob. Napuna din ng mga nagmamasid na ang mga delegadong ito ay may malalalim na kili-kili at hindi makatingin nang tuwid sa mga tao.

Mula nang gabing iyon hanggang sa matapos ang seminar ang mga taga-Lucban ay nagsabit ng mga pansahog sa pagkain katulad ng bawang at paminta sa kanilang mga bintana. Ang mga bubungan ay nilagyan nila ng krus.

---

[65] Contributed by Rosalinda A. Villaverde, of Lucban, Quezon, who had it from Cirila Saludares, from the same town.

Nang matapos ang seminar at ang mga delegado ay
makauwi na sa kani-kanilang bayan, nagbalik ang katahimi-
kan ng gabi sa bayang iyon.

～

In 1930 a teachers' seminar was held in Lucban,
Quezon. All towns in Quezon Province sent delegates.
These were housed in the elementary school buildings a
kilometer from the town proper. The seminar lasted one
week. The night after the delegates arrived, the townspeople living near the school compound heard peculiar
noises of flying wings and the sound "Tik-tik-tik" from
the tiktik bird. It was a firm belief in the town that
whenever the tiktik was heard at night there was or
were aswang around.

The next night, some brave folks peeped out of their
windows when they heard the sound of wings. They
were horrified when they saw a flock of black-winged
creatures flying in the dark of the night. The creatures
had human heads but half of their bodies from the waist
down were missing. The people presumed that what
they saw were manananggal.

The following morning, the people of Lucban who
had charge of feeding the delegates observed them
closely. They noticed that some of the delegates refused
to eat spicy dishes and were very fond of *dinuguan*
[meat cooked with blood] and *inihaw-na-lamang-loob*
[roasted internal organs]. They also noticed that these
delegates had deep armpits and could not look directly
into other people's eyes.

From that night till the seminar ended, the Lucban
populace hung spices such as garlic and black pepper
outside their windows. They placed crosses on top of
their roofs.

When the seminar was ended and all of the delegates had gone home, the peace of night returned to the
town.

40. [PORTRAIT OF A VISCERA SUCKER][66]
Tagalog Text

Lumawig (nag-ani) ang kaniyang ama sa Pola, Oriental Mindoro. Siya ay nanuluyan sa bahay ng kaniyang pamangking si Hugo Kilayan na malapit sa isang punong balete. Ang anak nitong si Juanita, 8, ay matagal nang maysakit nguni't hindi nila alam kung ano ang kaniyang sakit. Isang hatinggabi, sila ay nakarinig ng malalakas na yabag, sa lupa ngunit hindi nila ito pinansin. Sumigaw si Juanita ng "Inay!" Nang sila ay lumapit, napansin nila na may sinulid na nakalawit sa tapat ng pusod ng bata na siya nitong itinuturo. Si Mang Hugo ay kumuha ng kawit at pinutol sa kalaghatian ang sinulid. May narinig silang pumatak mula sa bubungan at kinaumagahan ay nakita na lamang nila ang isang lalaking patay na may isa't kalahating yarda ang haba ng mga paa, sabog ang kilay at may tatlong sungot (pangil) magkabila. Sinasabi ng mga taga-Pola na ang nilikhang ito ay taga-bundok. Ito ay inilibing sa tabi ng puno ng balete at itinuring nila itong aswang.

Juanita's father went to Pola, Oriental Mindoro, to harvest rice. He lived in the house of his nephew named Hugo Kilayan close to a balete tree. A child of his, Juanita, 8, had long been ill but they did not know why. One time at midnight they heard a loud thud on the ground but they did not mind it. Juanita shouted, "Mother!" When they got near her, they noticed that there was a piece of thread hitched to the child's navel which she was pointing at. Mang [Uncle] Hugo took a hook and cut the thread in the middle. They heard a sound from the roof and next morning they saw a dead man with legs a yard-and-a-half long, scattered eyebrows, and three fangs on either side [of his mouth].

---

[66] Contributed by Alicia S. Sylva, of Makati, Rizal, who had it from Avelina Azucena 18, from Isla Verde, Batangas, Batangas, who in turn heard it from her father, Antonio Azucena, a carpenter from the same town.

People from Pola say that the one here portrayed was from the mountains. Him they buried beside the balete tree and marked him an aswang.

41. [THE LOST FETUS][67]
Tagalog Text

Mayroon kaming isang buntis na kapitbahay na pitong buwan na ang laman sa tiyan. Nagkaroon kami ng handaan upang mabatid ng lahat na ang nanay ko ang siyang magiging ninang sa binyag. Kinabukasan, pagkatapos ng handaan, bigla na lamang nawala ang laman sa tiyan ng babae. Sinabi nila na ang bata ay kinuha ng isang aswang na nakikitira sa kabilang bahay.

Minsan, matapos ang isang pasayaw sa aming bahay, ako'y lumabas sa batalan. Nakakita ako ng isang aswang na palipad-lipad sa itaas. May pakpak siyang tulad ng sa agila, halos limang dipa ang haba, at hanggang baywang lamang ang kanyang katawan. Paligid-ligid siya sa itaas ng bahay.

◈

We had a neighbor who had been carrying a baby in her womb for seven months. We had a gathering to celebrate her having a baby because my mother would be the godmother at the chirstening. The next day, after the gathering, the woman [was seen to have] suddenly lost her baby. It was said that the baby had been taken by an aswang who was living in the house after the next.

After a dance at home when I went to the *batalan* (an open porch above the back ladder), I saw an aswang flying about overhead, its wings like those of an eagle,

---

[67] Contributed by Titus P. Labrador, from San Narciso, Zambales, who had it from Helen Espino, of Sorsogon.

in length five fathoms, and his body up to the waist only. It kept circling over the house.

42. [THE ASWANG AND THE *POO*][68]
Waray Text

Didto ha amon bungto, may ada mga wakwak hadto.
Yana poo na la it may ada. Mahihibaroan mo nga it tawo
wakwak kon hiya nakaturog hin adlaw, ngan kon hiya igin-
kukurog kon nakaturog. An wakwak waray pako ngan tango
nga haglaba. Sugad la hiya hit yano nga tawo pero kon gab-i,
an iya mga mata makaharadlok. Hiya nagmamata kon gab-i.
Kon pinapatay niya it tawo, pinipitlok anay niya ngan iya
gin-u-utod it tiyan ngan kinakaon it atay. Nahihimo kanga
wakwak, kon makakaon ka hin iya kinaptan ngan danay kon
nakaturog ka, ginbubutangan niya it iya laway an imo baba.
Kumadto ka la ha albularyo kon karuyag nimo matambalan
ka. Matatambalan ka la kon waray ka pa kaon hin siwo, kay
kon kinaon ka na hin siwo diri ka na matatambalan. Kon an
wakwak nakita hin siwo, an iya baba ginlalaway. An tawo
nga nataponan na hin pagka-aswang, nakaon la anay hin
siwo, katima tawo na an sinusunod pagkaon. It albularyo
makakabulig la ha iya kon waray pa hiya pakakaon hin siwo.
Tatagan hiya hit albularyo hin mapait nga tambal nga
makakapagsuka ha iya. An laway hit aswang nakakatapon kon
tunga na hin bulan.

Didto ha amon may ada pa yana hin poo. An iya kahimo
sugad hin tawo ngan waray hiya pako ngan daku nga tango
sugad hit wakwak. An poo naulpot la kon bug-os an bulan.
Nakaruo hiya hin poo kon hiya harayo pa hit iyo balay ngan
kon matikaharani na hit iyo balay. Hiton ikaupat nga

---

[68] Contributed by Evelyn Lorenzo, from Mexico, Pampanga, who had it from Antonio Dula, a former houseboy from Laoang, Samar. Miss Lorenzo made this note regarding the reconteur: "He seemed to be very familiar with his story. I think this was because he had seen and experienced the events. His father had seen how an albularyo (medium) cures a contaminated person."

pagkuru-o niya, a-ada na hiya hit iyo balay. Kon magkiki-
nuru-o it poo ngan diri ka magmata, kukuhaon it iyo bata nga
gotiay. Kon magmata ka, diri niya makukuha it bata kay ma-
hahadlok hiya nga hiya patayon hit nagmamangno hit bata.
Kon makita ka hit poo nga nag-i-inusa-an ka la, papatayon ka
niya. Nahitabo na ini han ako dada. Suwerte la niya nga hiya
nagmata, kay kon waray kukuhaon han poo an iya bata.

In our town there were wakwak before. Now there
are only poo. You will know that a person is a wakwak
if he sleeps at daytime and if he shivers as he sleeps.
The wakwak has no wings or fangs. He looks like an
ordinary person but at night his eyes are very frighten-
ing to look at. He is awake at night. When he kills a
person, he strangles him with his bare hands and then
cuts the stomach and eats the liver. You may become a
wakwak if you eat anything he has touched; and sometimes when you are asleep he puts his saliva into your
mouth. If you want to be cured, you get an albularyo.
You can be cured if you have not yet eaten a chick; otherwise you cannot be cured anymore. When a wakwak
sees a chick, his mouth waters. A person who has been
contaminated eats first a chick, later he eats a human
being. The albularyo will be of help to him if he has not
yet eaten a chick. The albularyo will give him something
bitter to make him vomit. The saliva of a wakwak becomes contagious after a period of fifteen days or half a
month.

At present, in our place we still have poo. Like the
wakwak he has the appearance of an ordinary person,
and he does not have wings or fangs. The poo comes
out only when there is a full moon. He shouts "poo"
when he is still far from your house and when he comes
nearer your house. When he shouts "poo" the fourth
time, he is already in your house. If you are not awakened by his shouts, he will get your small child, but if
you are awakened, he cannot get the child because he is
afraid he might be killed by the one taking care of the

child. If the poo finds out that you are alone, he will kill you. This happened to my aunt. Luckily she was awakened; otherwise the child would have been taken by the poo.

43. [AN ASWANG TOWN MAYOR][69]
Tagalog Text

May baryo sa Capiz na ang mga nakatira ay halos pawang aswang.

Ang pamahalaan ay nagpadala doon ng pitong pulis upang magsiyasat. Ang mga pulis na ito ay pumunta sa alkalde at nakiusap na doon sila magpapalipas ng gabi.

Pinatuloy sila at ipinaghanda ng pagkain at ng silid-tulugan. Ang pitong pulis ay nag-usap na sila'y di matutulog at sa halip ay magbabantay.

Nang hatinggabi na, ang pinto ay nabuksan at may kunganong pumasok. Pinagtulungan nila yaong huluhin subalit mabilis na nakalipad.

Ang alkalde pala ay aswang din, isang manananggal.

Kinabukasan ay umalis na ang mga pulis, umuwi, at ikinuwento ang kanilang karanasan.

There was a barrio in Capiz where almost all the inhabitants were aswang.

The government sent seven policemen to investigate the matter. These policemen went to the mayor and requested that they spend the night in his house.

The mayor welcomed them and had food prepared for them. Their bedroom and bedding were also prepared. The policemen agreed among themselves that none of them should sleep that night and should watch instead.

[69] Contributed by Celia J. Marquez, from Iyam, Lucena City, who had it in Tagalog from Clarita Suela, a former housemaid from Pitogo, Jaro, Leyte.

At midnight the door of their room opened and someone got in. Together they tried to catch him but he flew off swiftly.

They found out that the mayor was an aswang too—a manananggal.

Next morning, the policemen left for home and narrated their experience.

44. [FATHER AND HIS *ANANANGGAL* CONCUBINE][70]
Tagalog Text

Talagang may paniwala ako sa mga aswang, sapagka't mismong tatay ko ang nakaranas na makasama ang mga aswang. Si Tatay ay may "Number 2", kung tawagin, na hindi niya nalalamang isang aswang. "Ananangal" kung tawagin ito sa amin. Mahal na mahal naman siya ng babaeng iyon. Sa pagseselos ni Nanay, naghiwalay muna sila ni Tatay. Nakisama si Tatay sa kanyang "Number 2." Kasama nila ang dalawa pang kapatid na babae nito.

Isang hatinggabi, nagising si Tatay at nakita niyang wala sa higaan ang tatlo. Sinubukan niya ang mga ito sa pangalawang gabi. Hinintay niya ang mga babae at nang bumalik ang mga iyon ay bukang-liwayway na. Noon niya nakitang putol ang mga katawan nito, lumilipad sa itaas ngunit wala namang pakpak. Hindi muna siya kumibo. Kunwari'y tinanong lang niya kung saan nanggaling ang tatlo. Sinabi naman ng mga ito sa kanya na nanggaling sila sa piyestahan. Tinanong ni Tatay kung bakit siya hindi isinama sa kanilang pamimiyesta. Idinahilan naman ng kanyang "Number 2" na baka siya magalit. "Sa susunod na pamimiyesta ninyo'y ipagsama ninyo ako," ang sabi ni Tatay sa kanila.

Nang pangatlong araw buhat nang sila'y magsama, naisipan ni Tatay na bumalik kay Nanay. Nang hatinggabi na'y may naramdaman siyang sumusundot sa likod niya na mula sa sahig na yari sa kawayan. Nanaog siya sa ibaba upang tingnan kung ano ang nandoon. Iyon palang tatlong babae ang nandoon at siya ay kinukumbida sapagkat sila raw ay pupunta na sa piyestahan. Sumama naman siya kaagad. Naramdaman niya na pumaitaas na lamang sila at parang naglalakad sa ulap. Putol na rin ang katawan ng mga babae ngunit siya ay katulad pa rin ng dati. Hawak-hawak siya ng

---

[70] Contributed by Vivian B. Manalo, from Pasig, Rizal, who heard it from Jovita Santileces, from Kabusas, Camarines Sur.

:atlo sa kamay na parang inaakay. Tumawid daw sila sa isang malawak na dagat. Sa kabila ng dagat ay mayroong isang maliwanag na lugar. Sinabi ng tatlo na doon daw ang kanilang pamimiyestahan. Iniwanan siya ng tatlo sa itaas ng puno ng suha, at sinabi sa kanyang titingnan muna kung tuloy ang piyesta. Pumunta na iyong tatlo sa loob ng bahay na malaki. May patay pala sa loob ng bahay na iyon kaya maliwanag. Ang ginawa ni Tatay ay bumaba rin at sinubukan kung ano ang gagawin ng tatlo. Nang makita niya ay nakataob ang tatlo sa ibabaw ng katawan ng patay. Ang mga ito ay hindi nakikita ng ibang tao, kaya't hindi nila ito pinapansin. Pagkakita niya'y bumalik siya uli sa itaas ng puno. Namitas siya ng suha at inilagay sa kanyang bulsa.

Nang madaling araw na ay binalikan na siya ng tatlo. Hawak-hawak siya muli pag-alis ngunit bigla na lamang silang bumagsak sa lupa. Tinanong nila kung bakit tila mabigat si Tatay kaysa dati at isinagot naman ni Tatay na puno ang bulsa niya ng suha kaya siya ay bumigat. Pinai-wanan sa kanya ng tatlo ang mga suha at baka raw sumikat ang araw ay hindi na sila makararating sa kanilang bahay. Iniwanan naman ang suha at tuloy na silang umalis.

Nang dumating sila sa bahay ay inusisa ni Tatay kung ano ang ginagawa noong tatlo sa ibabaw ng katawan ng patay. Isinagot naman sa kanya na inaamoy nila ito dahil sa napakasarap daw ang amoy ng patay. "Sana isinama ninyo ako sa patay," ang sabi ni Tatay.

Doon muna namalagi si Tatay. Wala pang dalawang gabi ay sinabihan na siya kaagad na sila'y mamimiyesta. Pinag-handa siya sa paglalakad, ngunit sinabi naman niya na lagi naman siyang nakahanda. Noong gabing talagang lalakad na sila ay nagdahilan si Tatay na hindi makakasama, dahil sa tila nalalaman na niya ang ginagawa nila. Tumuloy din 'yung tatlo. Ang ginawa ni Tatay ay pinagpalit-palit ang mga putol na katawan nila, kaya nang bumalik sila ay hindi na nila maitama ang kani-kanilang baywang sa tamang katawan. Si Tatay naman ay nagtago sa silong ng bahay. Sumisigaw ang babae sa paghingi ng tulong sapagka't mag-uumaga na. Palibhasa'y mahal din naman ito ni Tatay ay ibinalik na niya

sa dating lugar ang mga putol na katawan. Kunwari'y
ginawa niya ito sa pagtatampo dahil hindi siya inuuwian ng
pagkain ng mga ito tuwing sila'y namimiyesta. Ang babae
naman, sa pagmamahal sa kanya ay nangako na sa susunod
ay uuwian na niya si Tatay. Pinabayaan muna ni Tatay kahit
ano ang gawin ng tatlo dahil sa gusto pa niya silang
subukan.

Sumunod na hatinggabi'y nagpaalam uli ang mga ito.
Pagbalik ay may dala silang balutan. Nang makita nilang
natutulog pa si Tatay ay itinago muna ang balutan sa
iskaparate. Kinaumagahan ay itinanong ni Tatay ang dala
nila para sa kanya. Dahil sa antok ay si Tatay na lamang ang
pinakuha nila ng balutan sa iskaparate. Nang buksan ni Tatay
ang iskaparate ay nagulat siya nang makita niya ang dala-
wang paa ng bata na nasa balutan. Habang natutulog ang
tatlo ay tumawag siya ng pulis at ipinakita ang mga paa ng
bata. Dinakip ng pulis ang tatlong babae at sila ay ikinulong.
Wala na silang panakot na makakawala o makalilipad sa-
pagkat ang langis na ipinapahid nila bago lumipad ay itinago
ni Tatay at hindi nila nadala nang sila ay dakpin. Sa madali't
sabi, ang langis na ito ang nagbibigay sa kanila ng
kapangyarihan.

Pagkalipas ng tatlong buwan ay namatay na rin si Tatay.

I really believe that aswang exist because my father
himself experienced being with the aswang. My father
had a "Number 2" whom he did not know was an
aswang. They are called *ananangal* in our place. He was
very much loved by this woman. Because of my
mother's jealousy, my parents separated and he went to
live with his "Number 2." With them were two sisters of
the woman's.

One midnight he awoke and saw that the three were
not in their beds. He observed them the following night.
He waited for the women and when they came back it
was dawn. It was then he saw that they had cut bodies
and they were flying in the air but had no wings. At

first he kept quiet. He just asked the three where they had been. They answered that they had been to a fiesta. My father then asked them why they did not invite him to join them. His "Number 2" reasoned that he might get angry with them. "Next time you go to a fiesta let me join you," my father told them.

The third day after he joined his concubine, my father decided to go back to mother. At midnight he felt something pricking his back through the bamboo slats in the floor. He went downstairs to see what it was. He saw the three women there and they invited him to join them to a fiesta. My father joined them immediately. He noticed that they just rose and seemed to be floating among the clouds. He alone was complete in body parts and the others were only from head to waist. The three held him by the hand to prevent him from falling. They crossed a wide sea. On the opposite side of the sea there was a well-lighted place. The three women told him that was the place of the fiesta. The three left him first on top of a pomelo tree and told him that they were going to verify if the fiesta would be held as scheduled. The three entered the big house. He discovered that there was a corpse inside the house, and that's why the house was well lighted. He climbed down from the tree and observed what the three were going to do. He saw the three head down on top of the cadaver. The other people could not see them, so they did not pay attention to them. After seeing that, he went back to the top of the pomelo tree. He picked some fruit and placed them in his pocket.

At dawn the three came back. Again they held him by the arms, but when they started to fly they fell to the ground. The three asked him why he was heavier than before and he answered that his pocket was full of pomelos which made him heavy. The three told him to leave the pomelos because the sun might rise before they got home. He left the pomelo and they left.

When they arrived home, Father asked them what they had done on the body of the corpse. They answered that they had smelled it because the smell of the corpse was very sweet. "You should have let me join you," replied Father.

In the meantime, Father continued staying with them. Not two nights later the woman gave him notice that they would go to a fiesta, and he said he was always ready. On the night they were leaving, father gave an alibi that he could not go with them because he had an idea of what they were going to do. The three went ahead. When they were gone, my Father went to the place where their lower bodies were hidden and interchanged the positions of the bodies so that when the women came back they did not know which lower half to attach their waists to. Meanwhile, Father hid under the house. The women cried for help because the morning was coming. Since Father loved her (his concubine), he placed again the half-bodies in their right positions. Father pretended that he did this because the women did not bring any food for him when they went to fiestas. The concubine, because of her love for my father, promised that they would bring him food the next time they went out. Father let them do all they wanted because he wanted to observe them further.

The next midnight, they said they would leave again. When they came back, they had a bundle with them, and when they saw that Father was sleeping, they placed it in the closet. In the morning Father asked them if they were able to bring something for him but because they were too sleepy, they just let Father get the bundle from the closet. Father was astonished when he opened the closet and saw that the contents of the bag were the legs of a child. He called the police while the three were asleep and showed them the legs. The police arrested the three women and jailed them. They had no means of escape because the oil that they rubbed on their bodies before flying was hidden by Father before they were arrested. In short, this oil gave them their powers.

After three months, Father also died.

45. [PUNISHMENT FOR A VISCERA SUCKER][71]
Waray Text

Han olitawo pa ako may-ada wakwak did to ha Cogon an ngaran he Mara. Damo an nasering nga hi Mara in para wakwak han mga bag-o nga anakan didto hadto nga lugar. Usa ka adlaw may-ada bag-o nga anakan nga namatay kay guin wakwak kono ni Mara. Guin higot ha barsa ngan iguin pasaog han carabao hasta nga namatay. An mga tagabaryo diri na kontento salet era guin labog ngadto ha lunayan han carabao. Nabuhi liwat hi Mara. Nahadluk an mga tawo era guin bayaan hasta nga namatay wala didto ha ligid han lunayan.

When I was still single there was a wakwak in Cogon whose name was Mara. Many said that Mara was the cause of the death of many mothers who had newly given birth there. One day a mother who had just given birth died because it is said she had been *wakwacked* by Mara [her blood was sucked out]. The barrio folks went to the house of Mara and tied him and mounted his body on a sled and had a carabao pull him over rocky ground. The barrio people were not yet content, so they dumped him into the mud where the carabaos wallowed. They said that Mara became alive again. The people were scared, so they left him there until he finally died.

46. [THE *WUWUG*][72]
Tagalog Text

Si Mang Juan ay may dalawang anak, si Jose at si Pedro. Isang gabi, si Pedro at si Mang Juan ay nangisda saman-

---

[71] Contributed by Marcelina Badiable, from Carigara, Leyte, who had it from Joaquin Badiable.

[72] Contributed by Alicia S. Sylva, of Makati, Rizal, who had it from Marilyn Rulona, a sixth grader from Calapi, Bohol, who in turn heard it from her late grandfather, Tidoy Rulona, a farmer from Binugawan, Calapi.

talang si Jose ay naiwan sa bahay. Kinakausap ni Pedro ang ama niya at nang lingunin niya ito ay nakita niya ang ulo nito na nakakabit ang bituka na kumikislap na animo'y isarg libong alitaptap na may ilang talampakan sa kanyang ulunan. At napagtanto niya na ang kanyang ama ang wuwug na nababalitang umaaligid sa hatinggabi. Pinanatili niya itong lihim nguni't nakita rin pala ito ng dalawang kaibigan ni Pedro na galing sa panghaharana. Naglagay sila ng sampung alimasag sa katawan ng wuwug. Nang kumabit ang wuwug sa kanyang katawan ito ay nangisay nang nangisay hanggang namatay. Nguni't bago siya namatay, inihabilin niya kay Pedro ang kaniyang pagka-wuwug, sa kabila ng pagtanggi ni Pedro. At si Pedro, dahil sa malaking kahihiyan sa mga kababayan at sa dahilang ayaw pumatay, ay nagpakalunod sa kumunoy.

Si Jose na kanyang kapatid ay nagtitinda ng balinghoy sa palengke. Walang bumibili ng kanyang tinda kung mahal na araw sapagkat paniwalang sa mga panahong yaon ay lumalabas ang mga wuwug.

⤫

Mang Juan had two sons, Jose and Pedro. One night Pedro and Mang Juan went fishing while Jose stayed home. Pedro was talking to his father, and when he turned to him he saw his head with the intestines dangling from it, shining like a thousand fireflies just a few feet above him. And he realized that his father was the wuwug rumored to be going around at midnight. He kept it a secret but Pedro's two friends who came from serenading saw it, too. They put crabs into the wuwug's body. When the wuwug joined his body, he wiggled and wiggled until he died. But before he died, he gave his wuwug-ness to Pedro, much against Pedro's wishes. And Pedro, because of great shame and not wanting to kill anybody, drowned himself in quicksand.

Jose, his brother, sells *balinghoy* [cassava cakes] in the market. Nobody buys his merchandise during Lent because it is the belief that during this time wuwug appear.

47. [A VISCERA-SUCKING
MOTHER-IN-LAW][73]
Cebu-Visayan Text

Sa akong nadungog sa mga katigulangan sila nakakita ng mga wakwak. Sa ilang mga estorya mao kini ang akong nadungog.

May usa ka familia nagapuyo sa usa ka baryo. Ang familia may usa ka ambungang dalaga ug inila sa mga kaulitauhan. Tungod sa kaguapa sa dalaga may usa ka ulitawo nga nabihag ug kini taga laing lugar. Daghan ang ning tambag sa ulitawo nga dili mangulitawo sa dalaga tungod sa pagkawakwakon. Apan wala magpatuo ang ulitawo ang dalaga ug ang ulitawo nagkadayon ug nagminyo. Sa ilang pagmuyo daghan siyang nakitang katingalahan ug sa pagkatungang gabi-i pirming mawala ang inahan sa dalaga. Usahay iyang makitang magkulob ug dayon molupad.

Tungod kay tigulang na ang inahan ug himalatyon kini wala dayon mamatay kay duna siya'y bu-ot ibilin sa babaye. Kini mao ang usa ka butang para ibilin ang pagkawakwakon. Tungod sa dakung kalo-oy sa babaye sa inahan kini iyang guidawat kay kuno kong dili niya dawaton kining inahan pirming mag-antus kung walay modawat sa iyang guikoptang pagkawakwakon. Ug sukad niadto ang babaye na usab ang nahimong wakwak.

From my grandparents I have heard many stories about aswang. Among many, I heard this story:

There was a family in a small village known as having the blood of aswang. There was a beautiful lady in this family and many wanted to court her. There was a man from another village who had seen the lady and wanted to marry her. But many people advised him not to marry her. The man did not believe what the people said to him so he married her. After their marriage the

[73] Contributed by Corazon Manuel, from Bangued, Abra, who collected it from Francisco Alforque, a farmer from Naga, Cebu City.

young couple lived with the family of the girl. Not long after their marriage, the man noticed something. At first the man did not pay attention to this. But there was a time when he saw his mother-in-law bowing down through the floor, and at mignight flew.

The mother-in-law was already so old that her life was very much conditioned between life and death. If her package of being an aswang could not be given to somebody, the dying mother would suffer much. So the wife of the man received the package, and the husband also noted the same events had happened to his wife. At midnight she was always out looking for a victim. And in the following morning, the whole town were puzzled over what had been the cause of people's death.

48. [ONE NIGHT IN A CAPIZ BOARDING HOUSE][74]

While I was in Iloilo, I met a friend, Ernesto Aguas, from Manila. He is a salesman connected with the maker of Listerine antiseptics. We celebrated our meeting. During the dinner we talked about our lives in Manila and almost everything else until finally we talked of where we were going to go after we finished our assignment in Iloilo City. Aguas pointed out to me that just in case I'd be assigned in Capiz, I must be careful about the aswang. I was a little bit surprised because that did not sound like Aguas. I had known him as a carefree and fun-loving guy who did not believe in superstition. I told him that he must be joking but he said he was not.

Still not believing, I asked him to relate what had happened that made him believe in the aswang.

---

[74] Contributed by Salvador M. Comprado, of Lilio, Laguna, who had it in English from Pedrito Ardieta, former auditor of an appliance firm and who in turn had it from Ernesto Aguas, a former salesman.

He told me that while he was stationed in a town in Capiz which he preferred not to name, he had a most horrible experience. Because of his work, he had to spend two days and nights in a boarding house with a fellow salesman. He had been warned beforehand to be careful and to bring something to protect himself from the aswang. He had laughed it off and said, "This is the Jet Age. Aswang do not exist."

And so with a jolly heart they proceeded to their destination. They reached the town first hour in the morning and went to the boarding house they were supposed to stay in. The house was owned by a friend of his fellow salesman's. Upon knowing that Aguas was new to the place, he was instructed not to say anything or mind anything unusual. Aguas was amazed, but his fellow salesman told him to be quiet.

When they reached their room, his fellow salesman explained everything. He told his friend why he had not told him before. He might not have come with him if he had. "Anyway the aswang is harmless," his friend told him. "Just pretend not to see anything unusual and nothing will happen to you."

So, bearing that in mind, they went on plying their trade that day.

When night came they went home. However, Aguas did not have any appetite because of what his friend had told him. He just went to bed with a bottle of soft drinks and some biscuits. Before retiring to bed, they were advised to close the windows and lock the door. By this time Aguas had already controlled his nervousness. He told his friend that he who believed in aswang did not have enough belief in God. However, they locked the door but he told his friend to leave the windows open, for it was quite warm and the windows were screened anyway.

At about one o'clock, Aguas felt that somebody was staring at him. He opened his eyes and looked around. At the window he saw an old woman, the lower part of her body missing, staring at him, her graying hair standing up and with her lips open in a devilish grin. Her eyes were bloodshot and big.

He was frightened and he tried to scream but nothing came out of his mouth. He tried to wake his companion up but he could not move. He tried to close his eyes but couldn't.

After a couple of minutes, the aswang flew away. He was perspiring profusely. He called his friend and was surprised to hear his own voice. Then Aguas told his friend his own experience. That night Aguas was not able to go to sleep and he just sat in bed till morning.

At breakfast he was about to tell the owner of the house what had happend but he was astonished at the portrait he saw in the dining room. It was the portrait of the landlord's mother and looked exactly like the aswang he had seen.

The landlord guessed what happened to him that night and told him it was his mother and not to worry about her because she couldn't disturb them any longer.

After breakfast, Aguas went back to the city.

49. [ASWANG AT HOME ON A FRIDAY][75]
Kinaray-a Text

Sa amon nga ginaistaran, bisan indi Capiz, ay madamo ang aswang labi na gid sang peacetime. *Ang amon caupod sa balay nga si Manang Lucing ay indi gid magpati sa mga aswang cag wakwak. Pero ang hambalunan sang mga tawo sa amon, si Julia cono nga amon casimanwa ay usa ca wakwak.*

Usa ca adlaw sang Biyernes, nag-adto si Manang Lucing sa balay ni Julia kay manghulam cono siya sang mga dra-wing para sa pamurda. Mga alas-sais na sang gab-i sang magabot siya. Nagpanoktok anay siya pero wala gid sing nagsabat. Pero indi man nakatrangka ang puertahan. Nag-

---

[75] Contributed by Lourdes Calibjo, from Dinalupihan, Bataan, who had it from Salvacion Balonon, a housemaid from Rumbag, Antique.

*adto siya sa sulod sang balay. Sang wala man ca tao, gin
abutan niya ang isa ca puertahan cag iya gid nakita si Julia
nga nagapungco sa isa ca dook sang cuarto cag ang iya nga
ulo ay nasa salug, nga daw naga pangadi.*

*Te, nagpalapit siya cag sang kuhaon niya cag gintaas ang
ulo ni Julia ay iya natan-awan ang buhok nga madamul cag
matig-a nga daw cuerdas sang gitara, ang mata cono ni Julia
ay daw sa bukaw, cag nakita ni Manang Lucing ang iya gaya
sa mata ni Julia nga nagabaliskad. Cag sa iya kilid ay may isa
ka botelya sang lana. Te nahadloc siya nagdalagan. Indi na
cono siya magkadto sa balay ni Julia liwat.*

Where we live, though it isn't Capiz, there are many
aswang, especially during the peace time [before World
War II]. Our neighbor, Manang Lucing, didn't believe in
aswang or wakwak. But one of the people in our place,
Julia, was said by many people to be a wakwak.

One Friday Manang Lucing went to Julia's home in
the fields to borrow an embroidery design. It was six
o'clock when she got there. She knocked at the door but
nobody answered. But the door was not locked. She
entered the house. Since nobody was there, she opened
one of the doors and saw Julia sitting in the corner with
head down on the floor as if she were praying.

She got near and pulled Julia's head up, and she saw
that Julia's thick hair was as hard as guitar strings, her
eyes were said to be like those of the owl, and Manang
Lucing saw her image inverted in Julia's eyes. And
beside Julia was a bottle of oil. She was very scared and
ran. She never went back to Julia's home.

(CONTRIBUTOR'S NOTE: Asked if Julia was still alive,
the informant said yes, she was old now but people
never saw her out of the house on Fridays. Informant's
father said that Friday was the day when the wakwak
wiped the oil off their bodies.)

Witch Legends

50. [BECAUSE OF FISH SAUCE][76]
Iloko Text

Ni Ardo ken ni Merced ket agararamidda ti boggoong ket
ti aramidenda nga boggoong dilis. Adu ti gumatang kadakuada ta isu da ti agararamid. Maysa nga aldaw, adda dua
nga baket a napan diay balay da nga dumawat ti boggoong.
Ket ni Apo Solang ket dakdakkel ti botelya na ngem ni Apo
Upeng. Nagawidda ngarud. Kinagabigatanna, ni Ardo ket
saan a makakuti ti sakit ti tiyan na isu nga impan ni Merced
diay ospital ngem kuna diay doctor nga sakit ti tiyan laeng
isu nga inyawid ni Merced diay balay da ket nagbituk ti
arbulario. Nangala diay arbulario ti baso nga napno ti danum
ket nakitana ti rupa ni Apo Upeng ket idi kasaona, timek ni
Apo Upeng manen ti nanggegna. Kinagabitanna, pinaisbu
diay arbulario ni Ardo ket rimmuar ti maysa nga bote nga
bogoong ket naimbangan.

Ardo and Merced make bagoong (fish sauce) from
anchovies. Many buy bagoong from them because they

---

[76] Contributed by Evangeline Gonzales, of San Fernando, La Union, who
had it from Merced Flores, from Canaoay, San Fernando, who in turn heard it
from her husband, Ardo Flores, a fisherman in the same town.

make it themselves. One day two old women went to their house to ask for bagoong. But Apo Solang had a bigger bottle than Apo Upeng.

The following day Ardo couldn't move and he had a stomachache and Merced took him to the hospital but the doctor told them he had only a stomachache and Merced took Ardo back to their home and she looked for an arbulario. The arbulario took a glass of water and in the water he saw the face of Apo Upeng. When he talked to Ardo he heard the voice of Apo Upeng. The following morning he told Ardo to urinate and when Ardo did so, he urinated one bottle of fish sauce and was cured.

51. [POWER OF A *MANGGAMOD*][77]
Iloko Text

Daytoy nga estorya ket nangngegko iti kaprobinsiyaak maipangguep ti manggagamod ngem kasla saan a nakappapati aglalo ta idi agisestorya agkatkatawa. Uray no kasta, pinaneknekan ti maysa a kailianna a daytoy nga estorya ket pudno. Ti estorya ket kastoy:

Dagiti tao ditoy nga ili ket agsidsiddaawda iti maysa a familia ta saanda nga al-aladan ti minulaanda uray agdindinamag ti adu nga agtatakaw iti rabii. Kasta unay ti siddaaw dagiti umili agsipud ta dagiti sanikua daytoy a familia ket saan a makutkuti. Dagiti agnaed agdillawda ket nagbalinda a matmataan dagiti tattao iti amin a pappapan-anda. Pinalpaliiwda daytoy a kustombre dagiti kaillianda. Awan ti mayat a makisao kadakuada. Maysa a rabii, adda nabartek a napan agtakaw iti minulaan iti nasao a familia. Ngem daksang-gasat ta kimpet metten iti bunga nga immuna nga iniggananna.

Dimteng ti agsapa, napan diay tatang ti daytoy a familia idiay minulaanda ket nasarakanna diay agtatakaw a nakakapet iti bunga diay kayo, ket dumawdawat iti kaasi kenkuana. Ket

[77] Contributed by Manolito Cartas, from Agoo, La Union, who had it from Felix Comboy, a conductor in the Philippine National Railways, from Agoo.

daytoy nga akinkukua iti mula saan a nakaunget no di ketdi
nangala iti sanga ti kayo ket binauna daytoy nga agtatakaw
kas tanda ti pinnakapakawanna. Naikkat ti pannakaikapetna
ket inkarina a saannanton a pidpidduaen daytoy nga inara-
midna.

Daytoy a pasamak nagrakurak iti intero nga ili (Agoo, La
Union) ket daguiti agtatakaw a nakadamag maipangguep iti
daytoy a napasamak ket saandan a pinangguep nga serken ti
pagnaedan dagitoy a manggagamod a inggana itatta saan a
makutkuti dagiti sanikuada.

❦

This story that I gathered from a provincemate of
mine regarding the ability of a manggagamod is some-
what incredible, especially because when he related it he
was laughing. However, the story of this friend of mine
was substantiated by his townmate who said it was true.
The story went this way:

The people in this town were wondering why a
certain family was not fencing their orchard though it
was well-known that there were many thieves at night.
Much to the surprise of the people in that place, the
possessions of the said family remained untouched. The
residents wondered why this was so. The family were
the center of attraction wherever they went. This family
resented the attitude of the people very much. Nobody
talked with them. One night an intoxicated fellow dared
to steal some of the fruit on the trees owned by the
family. Unfortunately the thief was attached to the very
first fruit which he grasped.

In the morning the head of the family went to visit
his orchard and found the thief still attached to the fruit
and begging mercy from the owner. The owner never
got angry; he took a branch of the tree and whipped the
trespasser as a sign of forgiveness. The thief was
detached from the fruit and he promised that he would
not repeat what he had done. News of this event spread
throughout the town (Agoo, La Union) and thieves who
heard the information never attempted to trespass the
dwelling place of the manggagamod and until now the
property of this family remains untouched.

52. [THE *MANANANEM*][78]
Pangasinan Text

Agawa ya diman ed baleymi nen mantaonak na 19. Say
negosiomi so manlakoy belas. Amayamay so kakumpitensiami
ed sayan negosio. Lapod maong ya pi-aarap ed saray
parokianos, matalagpit dan dayo-ey puestomi. Lapod saya,
sinibletan day inak.

Sakey ya ngarem si inak biglan ansakit so eges da.
Inawitan miray doktor, balet agda natambal may liliknaen nen
inak. Diad loob na sakey simba sinansakey min inawit iray
doktor balet agni nakal so sakit nen inak. Saray amistades mi
inbaga ra ya atanemay inak. Agkami manisia ed tanem, balet
diad pannonnonot mi kipapasen nen iyak, angawit kamin
siansiay albolario. Si albolario sinuwi toy inak. San say
inbaga to so ataneman ira.

Kangel nen amak ed saya, insukbit toy pusil to tan nila to
may saksakey ya manananem dimad baleymi tan inbagada ya
pateyenda tan poolan day abong to no agto ekaley intanem tod
si inak.

Inmonor met si manananem. Kasabi tod mad sikami,
nandasal insan to inapaplus so eges nen inak. Kasanlilikna
nakal may sakit na eges da tan linmigsa ra.

Akikasi may nanananem ya agdala sasakitan ta ibaga to
no siopa so nanpatanem ed si inak. Pinmaway ya sakey ed
samay kakompitensia mid negosio so nampatanem.

This happened in our hometown when I was 19
years of age. Our business was selling rice. We had
many competitors but then we were not affected because
of my mother's good public relations with our
customers. Because of this, my mother was bewitched.

One afternoon, my mother had a sudden stomachache. We called for a trained doctor but he could not do

---

[78] Contributed by Erasmus U. Neric, from Calasiao, Pangasinan, who had
it from Domingo T. Corpuz, from Barrio Magaspac, Urdaneta, Pangasinan, and
now a rice dealer in Sampaloc, Manila.

anything to help my mother from what she was suffering from. For a week one doctor after another was called but still the pain was with my mother. Our friends told us that my mother was the victim of a manananem. We didn't believe this but then we asked the help of an herb doctor. The result of the herb doctor's examination was that she was the victim of a manananem.

Upon hearing this, my father sent for the one and only known manananem in our place, and he threatened her with death if he did not cure my mother. The manananem obeyed. When they arrived at our house, he stood in front of his victim and uttered words and massaged my mother's belly. Minutes later my mother's stomachache was little by little lessened until it was completely gone. Then she began to show signs of comfort.

The manananem begged my father not to harass him and then told us that one of our business competitors was the instigator of the witchcraft.

53. [REJECTED SUITOR HIRES IGOROT MANGGAGAMOD][79]
Iloko Text

Idi 1960 adda nagarem ken ni Manang Mer a maysa nga Instsik, ni Vicente, ken maysa a Filipino a taga Pozorrobio, Pangasinan, ni Prangan. Daguitoy a dua, nabayagda a nagarem ngem ni Vicente ti nagasat a sinugnatan ni Manang. Nakaunget unay ni Prangan, isu a napan iday Baguio ket dimmawat ti tulong diay gayyemna nga Igorot. Impagamodna ni Manang; nabayag a nagsakit ni Manang. Adda oras a a napudot unay ti bagina, ken adda met oras a kalambrien. Adu ti doktor a nangipananmi, ngem saan met a naagasan, isu nga inayaban ni Inang ni Tatang Andring,

---

[79] Contibuted by Norma V. Esposo, from Canarvacanan, Binalonan, Pangasinan, who had it from Estrella Cabay, from the same town, who in turn heard it from her sister Maria.

*maysa nga arbularyo. Adda buto nga ikabil ni Tatang Adring
iti ima ni Manang ket nagriaw ni Manang ken nagsilap
dagiti matana. Binaot-baotda ni Manang agingga idi
imbagana nga, "Siak ni Prangan, saan dak a malmalluenen ta
nasaket unay, saankon a rangranggasan ni Mary ta agasak."
Nangala ni Manang iti katayna ket inyaprosna idiay tiyanna.
Pagammuan latta, timmacder ni Manang ket kinunana,
"Apay? Ania ti naaramidko?" Nanipod idin saanen a
nagsakit isu na. Kinuna ni Tatang Andring a diay
nabaddekanna a daga inkabelda iti bote ket indulinda idiay
siruk ti dalikan.*

In 1960 Manang Mer had two suitors—Vicente, a
Chinese; and Prangan, a Filipino from Pozorrubio, Pangasinan. These two courted her a long time but it was
Vicente who was answered [accepted] by her. Prangan
was angry so he went to Baguio and asked the help of
his friend, an Igorot. He had Manang Mer *gamod* [be-
witched] by his friend, so Manang was sick for a long
time. There were times when she had a very high fever
and times when she felt cold. We took her to many
doctors but she was not cured. So my mother called
Tata Andring, an herb healer.

Tata Andring placed a stone in her hand, and
suddenly the sick woman shouted and her eyes flashed.
She was whipped and chastised by Tata Andring until
she talked and said, "I am Prangan. Do not chastise me
any more because it is painful. I am going to cure Mer."
Manang took saliva from her mouth and placed it on
her stomach. Suddenly Manang stood and said, "Why
what happened to me?" From then on she was not sick
any longer. Tata Andring said that Prangan had taken
her foorprint, placed it in a bottle, and kept it under a
stove.

54. [THE WOMAN NOT GIVEN CREDIT][80]
Tagalog Text

Noong ako ay bata pa na mga siyam na taong gulang,
kami ay nanirahan sa baryo Kapanikiyan, La Paz, Tarlac.
Isang araw, sapagkat kami ay may tindahan, isang matandang
babae na kung magsalita ay napakatinis ang boses ang
nangungutang ng bigas sa aking tatay. Hindi siya pinautang
kaya't galit na galit siyang umalis.

Matapos ang isang araw, mayroong tumubo sa balikat ng
Tatay na animo'y maliliit na butil na nagkalat pagkatapos sa
kanyang dibdib. Noon una ay hindi namin pansin iyon
ngunit parami nang parami hanggang sa ang aking tatay ay
makaramdam ng pananakit. Ang nanay ko ay kaagad
naghinala sapagkat ang matandang babae ay alam ng lahat na
isang mangkukulam. Siya ay kumuha ng gas at pinuntahan
ang kubo ng mangkukulam. Binuhusan ng gas ang bahay at
sinabi sa mangkukulam na kapag hindi pinagaling ang tatay
ko ay susunugin ang bahay. Sa takot ng mangkukulam ay
sumama sa aming bahay. Hinaplos-haplos niya ang mga
tumutubong butlig sa katawan ng aking tatay at sinabi na
yaon ay mga singaw lamang na madaling maalis. Matapos
ang maghapon unti-unting lumubog ang mga butlig sa
balikat at pati ang kanyang lagnat ay napawi at tuluyang
siya ay gumaling.

When I was a child of nine years, we were living in
Barrio Kapanikiyan, La Paz, Tarlac. One day, as we had
a store, an old woman with a high-pitched voice asked
my father to give her rice on credit. My father refused
and the old woman left, very angry.

The next day there appeared on the shoulder of my
father several small hard growths scattered along his
shoulder and chest. At first we paid no attention to it

[80] Contributed by Norma V. Esposo, from Binalonan, Pangasinan, who had
it in Tagalog from Pagimolin Quirino, a former employee in the Treasurer's
Office, La Paz, Tarlac.

but the growth increased in number until my father felt some pain. My mother at once suspected the old woman since she was known by all as a witch. She took kerosene and went to the nipa hut of the witch. She poured the kerosene on the house and said that unless the witch cured my father, she would burn her house. In fear, the witch came with my mother to our house. She massaged the growths on the breast of my father, saying that those were mere outlets of heat and would easily disappear. After a day the growths disappeared little by little and likewise the fever until my father became well.

55. [THREE TALES ABOUT THE MANGGAGAMOD][81]

Witches Praying to Bat's Image

My cousin Fely married a medical student whose parents were believed to be manggagamod (witches). Prior to their marriage, her in-laws had maintained a high reputation because they were rich and were not witches then.

After the birth of Fely's first child a quarrel came between her in-laws and her own parents. This reached the barrio captain and that official tried to settle the dispute.

Fely and her husband were never reconciled. After the case, Fely divulged all that she knew about her in-laws. One of these was the following:

One midnight, her father-in-law and mother-in-law went downstairs carrying a lamp. Hearing rumors about the witchcraft of her in-laws, she decided to spy on them. She sneaked out to watch her in-laws, leaving her husband in their room. Her in-laws then went south of the long yard with the many fruit trees and spread out

---

[81] Contributed by Ma. Nelly R. Paronable, writing in English about her childhood experiences in Barrio Cayamanan, Urdaneta, Pangasinan.

and hung up a piece of cloth between the trees. This piece of white cloth was painted with a big image of a bat. Her in-laws then knelt and prayed before the image.

In the morning, Fely secretly told her husband but he did not believe her.

Maid Discovers Witch's Familiars

Another cousin has been a boardmate of a son of witches and met Olleng, their maid, who told her this account about witches. This maid was a relative of the witches and was herself suspected to be a witch. My cousin told her, "You might yourself be a witch!" To allay his suspicion, she told my cousin that whenever the father and mother left, at least one of their sons was left behind.

One time Olleng was cleaning the house. Below the *descanso* she saw a big clay pot, opened it, and found many species of insects. When she stooped and attempted to break it, the second son shouted and warned her that if ever she attempted to break it he would kill her. This was some years ago.

A Witch's Death

During a vigil, my aunt, a schoolteacher and wife of my paternal uncle, heard her cousin, a son of the dead witch, saying, "We never slept last night; our neighbors never slept, either." Their car went unlighted deep in the night. The said neighbor is a close relative, an aunt of the woman witch who died. Two members of this family, Don Mariano and his daughter Rose, a teacher, died of witchcraft. Rose died earlier. Don Mariano was found dead in the toilet.

After the death of these two, a quarrel between the witch and Don Mariano's family began because it was found that Rose and Don Mariano had been bewitched. This was years ago and today this educated family are a fanatical believer in witchcraft. In fact, their case with the witch's family is now in court.

Doña Eñang, the widow of Don Mariano, and her children hired many albularyos. I've heard they pay a lot of money to these. The last albularyo is said to have been paid to live with them. Barrio folks believe that the power of the albularyo is so strong that the witch cannot overcome it. There is a term, *balesen* in Ilocano, meaning that the hired albularyo will avenge the death of a member of the said family by making the witch sick or in some extreme cases die — that is if the herb doctor is good. What made people firmly believe that the power of the witch was overcome is that the witch, before her death, was taken to the Baguio General Hospital and had about sixty X rays of herself taken from different angles but the technician said she wasn't sick. In fact, she was exposed to the machine used to detect cancer.

People also said that when the man-witch was much worried over his wife's illness, he cursed their power and decided to throw away their pot of insects.

It is said that when the power of a witch is defeated, he can no longer employ magic to make people sick and thus will begin to be dizzy and finally dies.

56. [MANGGAGAMOD USING RICE GRAINS][82]
Iloko Text

Ni Lolong Marcelo ket nagamudan isu a natay. Kinuna kaniak ni Tia Josefa a ti inggamodda ket irik. Pinasapaanda ti maysa nga albolaryo ngem intuno dublienna nga umay agasan daydiay insapana ket agbalin nga irik. Nagan-ano kano ngem no bittakanda ket irik ti rummuar.

[82] Contributed by Wigberto N. Corpuz, from Agno, Pangasinan, who had it from Eleanor Corpuz, an elementary schoolteacher from Tidog, Agno, who in turn had it from Josefa Corpuz, of the same town.

My grandfather Marcelo was witched and therefore died. Aunt Josefa told me that he was witched by getting rice seeds into his body. A medium tended him, and on his second visit to dress the wound, the medium found out that my grandfather's medicine had been changed into rice grains. Pus had formed in it but if they pricked his wound with a pin, grains would come out.

57. [AN ASWANG LOVER][83]

Another story told by my friend was about two lovers. The man was not aware that the woman was an aswang. When his parents learned of this, they told him to leave the woman alone. The man immediately broke up with her for fear of being contaminated.

She did not know how to accept frustrations. His life did not last long. Before his burial his parents said a big black dog appeared during the middle of the night and visited the coffin and went away. His relatives said that his girlfriend, an aswang, had killed him and added that the aswang took revenge.

58. [AN EXORCISM][84]
Tagalog Text

Kararating lamang sa aming bahay si Auntie Norie mula sa ospital na kanyang pinanganakan. Mahusay na ang pakiramdam niya. Noon ding gabing yaon ay kasabay niyang dumating (sa amin) ang dati naming katulong na si Aling Maria. Humihiram si Aling Maria ng pera sa lola ko, ngunit ayaw siyang pahiramin (ng lola) dahil sa hindi siya nagbabayad ng utang. Hindi nagpakita ng pagdaramdam o sama ng

---

[83] Contributed by Ruth Cacayorin, from Bambang, Nueva Vizcaya, who heard it from Leopoldo Galam, then a college student from the same town.

[84] Contributed by Immaculada B. Blancaflor, from Santa, Ilocos Sur, who had it from Alice Bell, from Malolos, Bulacan.

loob si Aling Maria. Hiniling lamang niya na sa bahay siya magpalipas ng gabi sapagkat madilim na. Tumulong pa siya sa pagluluto ng aming pagkain at pinagsilbihan pa niya si Auntie Norie. Siya ang nag-akyat ng pagkain ni Auntie Norie.

Kinabukasan, noon, maagang umalis ng bahay si Aling Maria. Pagkalipas ng ilang sandali, nakaramdam si Auntie Norie ng masidhing sakit ng tiyan at siya ay dinugo. Naisipan ni Lola na tumawag ng albularyo sapagkat alam niya na kagagawan ito ni Aling Maria na isang mangkukulam.

Ang pagtawag sa albularyo ay kailangang pabulong lamang at pasenyas, sapagkat hindi dapat malaman ng mangkukulam na may albularyong darating. Pag nalaman niya ay makapaghahanda siya.

Pagdating ni Mang Puten, humingi siya agad ng tawas at isang baldeng puno ng mainit na tubig. Ang tawas na naging puti ay pinaghalong nganga at mga dahon. Humingi siya ng isang kawayan at pinalo niya nang pinalo si Auntie Norie. Sumigaw si Auntie Norie, "Aray, aray, masakit. Tama na!" Ngunit ang boses ay hindi sa kanya, parang basag at malayo ang pinanggalingan. Ipinagtuloy ni Mang Puten ang pagpalo kay Auntie Norie at sumigaw siya, "Umalis ka diyan! Kung hindi, hindi ako titigil. Para hindi ka lamang pinautang, ganyan na ang ginawa mo!" Patuloy na sumisigaw yaong tinig. Pagkatapos, sinabi ng tinig, "Tama na, aalis na ako." Hinimatay si Auntie Norie. Tinuruan ni Mang Puten si Lola na hugasan si Auntie Norie ng tawas at mainit na tubig sa balde. Gumaling si Auntie Norie, subalit wala siyang maalaalang mga palong tinanggap. Pagkaraan ng ilang araw, nagpunta si Aling Maria sa bahay at humingi ng tawad sa lola ko. Ang sabi niya, hindi sana niya gagawin yoon ngunit nagalit siya dahil hindi siya pinautang.

Aunt Norie had came home from the hospital after giving birth. She was already feeling well. That very same night a former helper of ours, Aling Maria, came to our house to borrow money from my grandmother.

80

My grandmother refused to loan her money, for Aling Maria never paid her debts. Aling Maria did not show any sign of resentment, however, but she only requested to spend the night in our house since it was quite late. She even helped in the preparation of our food and was extra solicitous over Aunt Norie. She even took up the food tray to Aunt Norie.

Early the next day, Aling Maria left. Soon after, Aunt Norie started complaining of severe stomach pains and she started bleeding. My grandmother decided to call an herb doctor since she knew that this was the work of Aling Maria whom she knew to be a witch. The calling of an herb doctor had to be done in whispers and with signs so the witch would not know that an albularyo was being called. If a witch knows that an albularyo will come, she can prepare herself. When Mang Puten, the albularyo, arrived, he immediately asked for *tawas* and a bucket of hot water. Tawas is a concoction of betel chew and herbs colored white. He asked for a piece of bamboo and repeatedly beat my Aunt Norie with it. Aunt Norie shouted, "Ouch, ouch—its painful! Enough!" But the voice was not hers and sounded cracked and it seemed to come from a great distance. Mang Puten continued beating Aunt Norie with all his might, at the same time shouting, "Leave or I will not stop. Just because you were not given a loan, you did this." The voice kept screaming and shouting. Finally, the voice said, "Enough! I am leaving now." Aunt Norie collapsed and lost consciousness. Mang Puten instructed my grandmother to wash Aunt Norie with the hot water and tawas in the basin. Aunt Norie got well and she could not remember the beating which she received. Several days, later Aling Maria came to our house and apologized to my grandmother. She said she was sorry but had only done those things because my grandmother had refused to lend her money.

59. [EXORCISM IN MANILA][85]

Years ago I had an opportunity to personally watch how they cured a person who was said to have been *nakulam* (bewitched). We—my sister and I—were in my brother-in-law's house in Sta. Ana, right here in Manila. Suddenly there was a commotion outside the door. Someone came to say that a woman next door was possessed by a mangkukulam.

We all ran to a house just a few doors away and we saw this woman, her hair disheveled and her eyes having a blank stare. An old man was scolding her and he was holding a knife. The woman was cowering in a corner of the room and she couldn't speak. She could only emit throaty sounds.

Then the old man with the knife approached the woman and told her sternly: "*Pag hindi ka umalis diyan e itatarak ko ito sa iyong dibdib. Sige, umalis ka na!*" (If you don't leave I'll thrust this into your chest. Go ahead! Leave!) This kind of talk went on for about five minutes and each time he brandished the knife in her face. Then she fainted and they made her sit down and drink water.

When she opened her eyes, the old man asked her if she knew the people around her and she called them by their nicknames, including my sister's mother-in-law.

Then we left.

60. [A LIFE TERM FOR BELIEF IN WITCHES][86]

This story was told to me by my grandmother, because in her locality in Taguig, Rizal, people still believe that witchcraft and mangkukulam really exist. Even professionals cling to this belief nowadays and

---

[85] Contributed by Edelmira T. Manikan, writing about her own personal experience.

[86] Contributed by Vivian B. Manalo, from Pasig, Rizal, who heard it from Anastacia Bilaw, a housewife from the same town.

cause the people to be so backward. Sometimes the witches are called *manggagaway*.

A neighbor had a beautiful daughter who was courted by a handsome young man. The girl was from Tipas and the boy was from the nearby barrio of Ususan, but they were from the same town, Taguig. The girl and her old folks did not like the boy, so there was no other thing for her to do but turn him down. The boy left, threatening revenge.

After a few days, the girl, Lucita, got sick with an ailment of no possible explanation. Sometimes her legs got swollen, then her stomach bloated, her eyes protruded, and her nose flattened. Even the doctors could not explain her sickness.

Her father heard that the man belonged to a family of witches. Angrily Lucita's father and brother searched for the boy. They burned his house and killed the persons they found inside. Killed were the mother, the father, and the boy.

The man's brothers came and were very angry. They filed a suit against the father and the son. They were sentenced to life imprisonment because of multiple murder for failing to present in court evidence that it was really the mangkukulam who did the evil thing to Lucita. Until now they are still in Muntinglupa[87] and Lucita became eventually insane.

61. [THE MAN WHO DERIDED A WITCH][88]
Catanduanes Text

Sa sarong barrio ning Huban, Sorsogon, may nag-estar na sarong gurang na babaye na pinagsasabing hocloban. Gabos tacot saiya kaya an gabos na magostuhan nia pinagsunod.

---

[87] Muntinglupa—a town in Rizal where the national penitentiary is located.

[88] Contributed by Ma. Yolanda R. Borjal, from Virac, Catanduanes, who had it from Salvacion Borjal, a government employee from Gubat, Sorsogon.

Sarong aldao igwang sarong lalake na dai nagtutubod sa huklob na nagduman sa pagbisita saiyang mga tugang. Nagtaram su lalake nin maraot manongod sa gurang na babae. Pinagtaraman siya kan nga tawo na mag-ingat sa saiyang pigtataram, pero dai sia nagtubod. Paka tapos ning sarong simana nagplano na siang maparibod, pero bago sia nakahale kinulugan sia nin tulac. Maski na sia pigbulong ning doctor dai sia naayaa. Sinabihan sia na maghagad nin tawad duman sa gorang na babaye. Kan premero dai sia nagtubod. Kan dai na nia matiosan su kulog naghagad guiraray sia nin tawad sa gurang na babae. Pinatawad naman sia kan gurang. Ang asin pighaplos siya sa tulac nin lutab, asin nahali so kulog. Pagpuon kaidto dai na nin nagtatsar duman sa gurang.

In a certain barrio in Juban, Sorsogon, there lived an old woman who was believed to know the craft of the *hoclob*. Everybody was afraid of her and tried to please her in all her demands.

One day a man who did not believe in the power of witchcraft visited his relatives. He uttered ugly remarks about her. He was told to be careful, but he did not heed the warning. After a week he decided to leave but before he could do so, he felt a terrible pain in his stomach. He received medical treatment but did not get well. He was advised to ask the forgiveness of the old woman. At first he would not believe the advice but when he could not stand the pain any longer, he sent for the old woman and begged her forgiveness. The old woman forgave him and applied her saliva on his stomach and the pain disappeared. From that time on, nobody ever uttered bad words against any old woman.

62. [A BARANGÁN'S SNAKE PETS][89]

Years ago, my sisters decided to spend a week's vacation in my aunt's place about five miles from our town. They arrived at 7:35 in the evening, and being tired after the long walk, they asked for some water. But when they raised their heads to sip the last drop, they nearly threw their glasses away because they saw a variety of snakes up in the ceiling. But my aunt said, "Stay calm, they won't hurt you, they are my pets." Because they couldn't stand the mere sight of them, after three days they went home.

The snakes were the pets of my aunt because she is a *barangán* . But she is gentle in every way. She stays with us for a week or two and makes friends wherever she goes. Her eyes are not sharp and the pupils are not long like a cat's. During Good Fridays, she always goes home prepared with the things she needs for events which are connected with her profession. She takes a gallon of oil to a cave and there she calls on all the spirits mentioned in her prayers. This oil she needs for healing wounds, skin diseases, snakebites, fractures, etc.

Once my brother asked her for some of it and she gave him a bottle with roots and oil in it, charging him to avoid any place and occasion whenever the oil bubbled. The oil is never consumed although it overflows. Unfortunately, he lost the bottle after ten years.

The identifying mark on a barangan is a circular black spot on her palate. This is believed to have been there since her birth.

---

[89] Contributed by Wenceslao R. Katindoy Jr., from Abuyog, Leyte, writing about a boyhood experience.

63. [THE SPEARED CAT][90]

In Abango, a small barrio in Leyte where we used to live, a man was suspected to be an aswang. His name was Julio. He and his family lived in the outskirts of the barrio near a small forest. Julio had an ugly face and reddish, bulging eyes. He had many cats for pets.[91]

A week after giving birth, my mother got sick. Julio, who used to pass by our house, would ask my father how Mother was. My mother did not get any better and grew worse instead. The albularyo said that she had been bewitched and suspected Julio to be the culprit.

One midnight a big cat called *laog* was seen by my father under the house, right under the place where my mother was lying down. My father got his bamboo spear and aimed it at the laog and hit his mark. The laog gave out a terrifying shriek and then died on the spot.

The next morning were told that Julio had died that same night.

64. [THE *UNGO* AND THE BUS DRIVER][92]
Cebu-Visayan Text

Ang akong igsuon, driver sa autobus. Tambok kaayo siya. Dako ang iyang tiyan. Pag-abot niya guikan sa viaje, nga nagdiskarga sa pasahero nga guikan sa siyudad, may babae nga ungo nga nagsugat sa iya. Unya gihampak siya ng gui-ingon nga, "Sus, pagkatambok baya nimo, kadako nimong tiyan." Sukad niadtong hitabo-a guikan sa paghampak adtong babae nga ungo, may gibati na siya sa iyang lawas. Kanunay nang maglabad ang iyang ulo hangtud nga nag-higda na siya

---

[90] Contributed by Marcelina Badiable, from Carigara, Leyte, who had it in English from her father, Joaquin Badiable.

[91] Cats as witches' pets or incarnation is a notion probably imported from Europe and is not native to the Philippines.

[92] Contributed by Felicisima B. Parilla, of Tuburan, Cebu, who had it from Antonio Esmero, of the same town.

sa banig. Ang iyang asawa dili mosugot nga patambalan sa
arbularyo kay ang gusto sa asawa nga doctor ang matambal.

Sigon sa sulti-sulti, dili man maayo ang doctor. Ang
makaayo kaniya kanang mga arbularyo sa bukid.

Unya kay wala man patambali sa arbularyo sa bukid,
doctor man ang nagtambal, namatay ang aking igsuon kay
ang doctor dili man mutuo sa ungo. Wala man kuno sa libro.

My brother was an autobus driver. He was very
stout. He had a big belly. When he arrived from his trip
and he had unloaded the baggage of the passengers who
came from city, a girl who was an *ungo* woman came to
greet him. Then she tapped him on his shoulder and
said, "[Je]sus, how fat you are, how big is your belly!"
Since that occasion when the ungo woman tapped him
on the shoulder, he felt something wrong with his body.
He always had a stomachache and headache until he lay
down on his mat. His wife didn't agree that he should
be whispered to [i.e., incantory phrases should be said
near him] by the herb healer because she wanted a
doctor to whisper to her husband.

According to belief, the doctor was not good. Those
who could cure him were the albularyo of the fields.

Afterward, since the herb healer of the fields failed
to cure him—only a doctor could cure him—my brother
died because the doctor did not believe in the ungo,
which he said were not in his books.

65. [WITCHCRAFT CURE WITH A BEVERAGE][93]
Tagalog Text

Ang Tiya Charing mo ay nakipag-away sa isa naming
kapitbahay. Kinagabihan, ang Tiya Charing mo ay sumakit
ang tiyan. Tumawag kami ng albularyo at pagdating niya ay

---

[93] Contributed by Miguel H. Benedicto, from Pasay City, who gathered it
from Arsenio E. Benedicto, a retired government employee from Villadolid,
Negros Occidental.

nagpakuha ng palangganang may tubig at kandilang may
sindi. Pagkatapos ay pinatakan niya ng kandila ang palang-
ganang may tubig, at pagkaraan ng ilang saglit, isang anyo
ng isang babae ang nabuo sa tubig. At tiniyak ng albularyo
na ang Tiya Charing mo ay nakukulam. Pinakuha kami ng
albularyo ng buntot page at hinagupit ang Tiya Charing mo
para daw palayasin ang masamang ispirito sa kanyang kata-
wan. Ngunit ang Tiya Charing mo ay nasaktan din.
Pagkatapos ay kumuha ang albularyo ng isang dahon, inilaga,
at pagkatapos ay ipinainom ang sabaw sa Tiya Charing mo.
At makaraan ang ilang oras, gumaling ang tiya mo.

Your Aunt Charing once had a quarrel with one of
our neighbors. When night came your Aunt Charing had
a severe stomachache. We called an herb healer and he
asked for a basin of water and a lighted candle. Then he
made the candle wax drift on the water and after a few
minutes the figure of a woman was formed. Then the
herb healer was sure that your aunt was bewitched. The
herb healer asked for a sting ray's tail and he whipped
your aunt with it in order to drive the evil spirit out of
her body. But your Aunt Charing felt the pain too.[94]
Then the herb healer took a leaf and asked us to boil it
and then made your Aunt Charing drink the water in
which the leaf was boiled. And after a few hours, your
Aunt Charing got well.

66. [A PECULIAR STOMACHACHE][95]
Cebu-Visayan Text

Kini daw si Tatay Ladingan dunay nakaaway nga ilang
silingan nga gidungog sa daghan. Nagtinobagay sila hangtud
milabay ang pila ka adlaw.

---

[94] She typically should not have.

[95] Contributed by Norma D. Jumilla, from Sta. Cruz, Davao del Sur, who had
it from her mother. The incident happened more than thirty years ago.

*Usa ka adlaw niana nagreklamo nga cono si anhing Tatay
Ladingan nga ang iyang tiyan gasakit, unya laing klase sa
sakit dili kay ordinaryo nga sakit sa tiyan lang. Unya kining
iyang tiyan nagdako pero wala may sulod. Kung hunas anag
dagat mogamay ang iyang tiyan pero kung taob gani modaku
pud ang iyang tiyan.*

*Lain pa niani magkalibang siya ug itom nga lapok. Unya
gipatambalan siya sa mananambal nga bisaya pero wala man
gyud siya maayo. Nisamot lang hinoon hangtod usa ka adlaw,
ana kay wala na siguro makaantos, namatay siya.*

This Tatay Ladingan had a petty quarrel with one
of his neighbors and it was heard by many. They exchanged words and the days passed.

One day Tatay Ladingan complained of his stomach
and that the pain was different from an ordinary
stomachache. Then his stomach grew big but there was
nothing unusual inside it. If it was low tide his stomach
would become small, but if it was high tide it became
big again. [This is called *paktol.*]

Other than this, he would excrete black mud. Then
he was taken to a common healer [*mananambal nga
bisaya*] but did not recover. Instead his condition
worsened until one day, perhaps because he could no
longer stand it, he died.

(CONTRIBUTOR'S NOTE: The children and relatives
believe that the neighbor whom he had quarreled with
might have grown angry and did it as a revenge. It's
hard to believe this but most of my relatives claimed it
was true because they saw it with their own eyes.)

67. [THE SNOBBISH GIRL AND THE PEDDLER][96]
Tagalog Text

Noong una'y hindi ako talagang naniniwala sa mga
mangkukulam, ngunit nang maging biktima ang aking anak
ay walang nalabi sa akin kundi ang maniwala. Nangyari ito
nang makipamista sa Ususan, Taguig, Rizal, kasama ng isang
kaklase, si Aurora. Maganda nga si Aurora pero suplada
naman.

Maraming nangaghilerang mga magtitinda nang sila'y
bumaba na sa dyip. Isang magtitinda ng balot ang
nagwikang, "Ineng, bumili ka na ng balot sa akin. Balot ito sa
puti, kasing puti ng iyong kutis. Ang ganda-ganda mo.
Siguro ang daming lumiligaw sa iyo." Sa inis naman ni
Aurora, nairapan niya itong lalaki at sinabing, "Aba! Sobra
naman ito, e. Ano bang pakialam mo? Nagtitinda ka lang,
akala mo kung sino ka."

Napatingin ng matalim ang lalaki. Nagyaya na agad si
Aurora sa kanilang pupuntahan.

Habang kumakain sila sa balkonahe ng bahay, ay
napatingin siya sa may pinto ng bakod. Nakita niya iyong
mama na nakatitig sa kanya. Umalis siya nang makitang
tumingin siya.

Bigla siyang nagyayang umuwi dahil natakot rin siya.
Pagdating sa bahay ay hindi ito mapalagay. Parang hindi
niya alam ang kanyang ginagawa at napakatalim tumingin.
Hindi ako makausap.

Isang araw ay tinanong ko siya kung siya ay may
dinaramdam. Sumagot ngunit naiba na ang boses nito. Tila
ba boses ng isang lalaki. Hindi ko muna ito pinansin.
Sinubukan ko muna siya. Napansin ko kung umupo siya sa
silya ay nakaangat ang paa niya sa sahig. Sa loob ng isang
araw ay hindi lamang isang beses kung pumasok siya sa
banyo. Sinundan ko siya at nakiramdam sa kanyang gagawin.
Narinig kong may parang kausap siya sa loob ng banyo at
dinidigahan siya. Bigla kong itinulak ang pinto upang ting-

---

[96] Contributed by Vivian B. Manalo, from Pasig, Rizal, who had it from
Antonio Benito, a plumber from Sagad, Pasig.

nan kung sino ang nasa loob. Wala namang tao, nakatingin si Aurora tila takot na takot. "Aurora, ano ba'ng nangyayari sa iyo? May nararamdaman ka ba?" ang tanong ko sa kanya.

Bigla na lang siyang umalis. Hindi ko na siya binagabag pagkatapos.

Kinabukasan dinala ko na siya sa isang doktor, ngunit wala namang masabi ang doktor tungkol sa karamdaman. Mayroon naman akong hipag na nagmungkahi ng albularyo na kakilala niya. Marami na raw iyong napagaling.

"Ayoko nga. Mamaya lalo pang lumala ang aking anak," ang sagot ko dito.

"Alam mo, Tonying, minsan may mga pagkakataong dapat nating gawan ng paraan. Pumayag ka na," ang paliwanag naman ng aking hipag.

Sinundo namin si Mang Inyong, ang nasabing albularyo. Pagdating niya sa bahay ay tiningnan niya ng diretso sa mata si Aurora. "Nakulam ho ang anak ninyo, Mang Tonying," ang wika niya.

"Ho! Paano hong nangyari?" ang tanong ko.

"Mamaya na kayo magtanong at pinauunahan kong huwag kayong makikialam sa ano mang gagawin ko sa kanya," ang wika ng arbolaryo.

Hindi na ako kumibo. Kumuha siya ng isang walis na may matigas na hawakan. May parang ibinulong pa siya at pagkatapos ay hinataw nang hinataw si Aurora. Awang-awa ako nang makita ko siyang namimilipit, ngunit nawala ang aking awa bigla siyang sumigaw na ang boses ay tulad sa isang lalaki. Wala namang makikitang latay sa katawan ni Aurora. "Tama na po, napipilay na ako!" ang sabi ng boses.

"Talagang pipilayin kita kapag hindi mo nilubayan ang batang ito," ang sabi ng albularyo.

"Opo, hindi na po ako muling babalik," ang sagot ng boses.

Si Aurora naman ay bumangon at pagkatapos ay humiga ulit at natulog.

"Hindi muna ako aalis. Hindi pa grabe ang dinanas ng walang-hiyang iyon kaya baka bumalik pa," ang sabi ang albularyo.

Pagkagising nga ni Aurora ay napansin namin na iba na naman ang ikinikilos nito.

"Ngayon ay makakatikim ka na ng talagang parusa mo," ang sabi ng arbolaryo. Nagpakuha ito ng pakpak ng manok. Binulungan niya ito uli. Inilagay niya ito sa pagitan ng kalingkingan ng paa ni Aurora. Pagkatapos ay kinalabit niya ito.

Isang napakalakas na sigaw ang lumabas. "Aray ko! Magang-maga na ang paa ko. Hindi na ako makalalakad," ang sabi ng boses.

"Matigas ka talaga. Bakit ayaw mong lubayan si Aurora? Ngayon hindi kita talaga patatahimikin," ang sabi ng albularyo. Ginalaw niya ang pakpak at nagpatuloy ang sigaw.

Pagkatapos biglang humupa ang boses at tuluyang nawala. Biglang bumangon si Aurora at nagtanong kung bakit maraming tao sa bahay at kung ano ang nangyari sa kanya.

Pagkaraan noon ay hindi na siya suplada. Ngayon ay may-asawa na si Aurora.

I did not believe in mangkukulam, but when my daughter became a victim, I was forced to believe in them. This happened when she, with one of her classmates, went to a fiesta in Ususan, Taguig, Rizal. Aurora was indeed beautiful, but very snobbish.

There were lines of peddlers when they got off the jeep. A balut peddler said, "*Ineng* (young lady), buy balut from me. This balut is as white as your complexion. You are very beautiful. Maybe you have many suitors." In Aurora's annoyance, she gave an angry look to the man and said, "Oh, this man is abusive. What business is it of yours? You are only a peddler and you pretend to be somebody."

The man looked at her ferociously. Aurora immediately told her companion that they should proceed to where they were going.

While they were eating at the balcony of the house where they went, she looked and saw the man looking fiercely at her. He left when he saw her looking at him.

She asked her friends that they go home because she was afraid. When she got home, she was uneasy. She did not seem to know what she was doing and she looked at people very sharply. She could not speak to me.

One day I asked her if she was feeling anything wrong. She answered, but a different voice came from her. It was like that of a man. I did not pay attention to this at first. I observed her. I noticed that when she sat on the chair, her feet did not touch the floor. She entered the bathroom more than five times a day. I followed her and kept alert for whatever she was going to do. From what I heard, she seemed to be talking with someone courting her. I suddenly pushed open the door to see who was there. No one was with her, but her look showed she was very afraid. "Aurora, what is happening to you?" I asked her. "Are you sick?"

She suddenly left. I asked no further questions.

Next morning I took her to a doctor, but the doctor could not tell what the matter was. I had a sister-in-law who suggested we better ask see an herb healer whom she knew.

"No. My child might grow even worse," I replied.

"You know, Tonying, there are times when we have to try all remedies. Better agree," my sister-in-law added.

We fetched Mang Inyong, the herb healer. When he got to our house, he looked directly into Aurora's eyes. "Your child is a victim of *kulam*, Mang Tonying," he said.

"What! How can such a thing happen?" I asked him.

"You question afterward and I am warning you not to interrupt me in anything I will do to her," the herb healer said.

I just kept quiet. He took a broom with a hard handle. He seemed to whisper something to the broom

93

and then began whipping Aurora. I pitied the girl very much when I saw her twisting in pain, but my pity subsided when the cry she gave out was that of a man. There were no welts on Aurora's body. "Stop it! I am going to be crippled!" the voice said.

"I will indeed cripple you if you do not leave this child," the herb healer said.

"I promise never to come back," replied the voice.

Aurora suddenly got up but lay down again and fell asleep.

"I'll not leave yet. I did not give him the fullest measure of punishment, so the shameless fellow may come back," the herb healer said. And indeed, when Aurora awoke, we noticed that she was acting funny again.

"Now you will feel the punishment you deserve," the herb healer said. He asked for a chicken feather. He whispered to it and place it between her smallest toes. Then he tapped the feather.

A very loud yell came out. "Ouch! My feet are swollen. I can't walk!" the voice said.

"You are really stubborn. Why do you refuse to leave Aurora? Now I'll not give you peace," said the herb healer. He moved the feather and the yells continued.

Then the voice softened until it vanished. Aurora suddenly rose and asked why there were so many people in the house and what had happened to her.

After that she was not snobbish any more. Now she has a husband.

Legends about Aswang
of Undetermined Category

68. [THE PRETTY WOMEN OF THE WOODS][97]
Iloko Text

Adda kano tallo nga nagpipintas nga babbalasang ken maysa nga lakay. Dagitoy kano babbalasang adda balay da idiay kabakiran. Daydiay lakay, idiay ili ti paggigiananna. Maysa nga aldaw daytoy nga lakay awan ti sidana ket napan idiay bantay nga agsapul iti frutas. Nakakita kano ti napintas nga balay ket immuneg tapno dumawat ti bassit laeng nga sida na. Awan ti nakitana nga tao ket nagsapul iti makan didiay nga balay ngem awan met iti makitana. Immuneg ti maysa nga kuarto ket nakakita iti nagpintas ken nalamuyot ti kudil na nga babai. Inasut na kano daydiay buneng na sana insina ti siket na sana inasinan diay sugat na. `Nakarurud daydiay lakay, pinurwakan na iti asin diay siket na. Daydiay bagina saan kanon nga nagsubli. Kalpasanna pimmanaw diay lakay nga dagos ta ammona nga adda pay dua nga babbae a castoy iti balay.

[97] Contributed by Wigberto N. Corpuz, from Agno, Pangasinan, who had it from Vilma Quiñola and Ising Quiñola, from Sabangan Norte, Agno.

There were said to be three exceedingly beautiful ladies and an old man. These ladies lived in the forest. The old man lived in the town. One day the old man had nothing to eat with his rice, so he went to the forest to look for fruit. There he saw a beautiful house; entered it to ask for food to go with the rice. But he saw no one. He proceeded to look for food in the house but saw nothing. He entered one room, and there he saw a very beautiful woman with smooth skin. He pulled out his bolo, cut her in two by waist, and salted the wound. He was angry and he tossed more salt on the woman's waist. Her body could thus never be whole again. After this he left at once because he knew there were two other women like her in the house.

69. [ASWANG DISGUISED AS A FRUIT][98]
Tagalog Text

Sa Olongapo, noong hindi pa ito siyudad, ay may isang uri ng aswang na nag-aanyong bayabas na malaki. Kapag ang mga batang naglalaro ay tatangkaing pitasin ito, ito ay biglang magiging malaking sawa at isusubo nito nang buong-buo ang mga bata.

In Olongapo before it became a city, there was a type of aswang that pretended to be a big guava fruit. When children at play tried to pick it, it suddenly turned into a big python and swallowed all the children whole.

[98] Contributed by Wilfredo N. Mananquil, of Calumpit, Bulacan, who heard it from Danilo Bonus, of Olongapo City, and who in turn heard it from Vivencia Castro, a former housemaid.

70. [THE ASWANG WHO CAME TO PLAY][99]
Tagalog Text

Sa amin ay may mag-asawa na matanda na. Sila ay
kinatatakutan pagkat, ayon sa marami, sila raw ay aswang.

Isang araw ay may taong nagkasakit. Ang mag-asawa ay
may ilang ulit na nagpabalik-balik sa bahay ng maysakit.
Pagkalipas ng ilang sandali ay namatay ang maysakit.

Isang araw ay naglalaro kami ng taguan. Ang mag-asawa
ay sumali. Galit na galit ako pagkat pag sila ang taya ay
hindi sila pumipikit kaya ako tuloy ang naging taya.

Hindi rin ako pumikit at sinundan ko ng tingin ang mag-
asawang magtatago. Gayon na lamang ang aking takot nang
makita kong ang mag-asawa ay kapwa naging pusa.

In our place lived an old couple. They were feared
by the people because many said they were aswang.

One day somebody got sick. This couple kept on
visiting the patient's house. After a while the patient
died.

One day we children were playing hide-and-seek.
The couple joined us. I was very angry because they
never closed their eyes whenever they were "It", and
they saw me hide, so I became "It".

I didn't close my eyes and I followed them to their
hiding place. To my horror I saw both of them change
into cats.

71. [AN ASWANG AT A PARTY][100]
Tagalog Text

Minsan ay nagbakasyon ako sa Sipocot, Camarines Sur.
Dumalo kami sa isang salusalo para sa kaarawan ng aking
kaibigang si Saling.

---

[99] Contributed by Celia J. Marquez, from Iyam, Lucena City, who had it from
Erlinda Dimaano, of San Cristobal, San Pablo City.

[100] Contributed by Celia J. Marquez, of Iyam, Lucena City, who had it from
Connie Capistrano, of the same city.

Ang may bahay ay naglagay ng walis na tingting sa puno ng hagdan upang huwag makapasok ang aswang.

Pagkalipas ng ilang sandali ay may dumating na magandang babae. Nagtaka kami kung bakit tumawag pa samantalang bukas naman ang pinto. Humingi ng paumanhin si Saling sa kanyang mga panauhin at nagtungo sa hagdan upang alisin ang walis.

Ayon sa ina ni Saling ay aswang daw ang babaing iyon. Nang kami ay kumakain na ay panay ang tingin sa akin ng nasabing babae. Ang mata niya ay parang nag-aapoy. Lumapit sa akin si Saling at sinabi na ayaw ng kaibigan niyang aswang ang kinakain ko pagka't may bawang.

Nang mag-iikasampu na ay dumating ang ama ng aswang upang sunduin siya. Iginagapos daw ngunit nakakaalpas din.

I once spent my vacation in Sipocot, Camarines Sur. We attended the birthday party of my friend Saling.

Saling's mother placed a coconut-midrib broom at the foot of the ladder so that no aswang could get in.

After a few moments a pretty girl arrived. We were much surprised why she still called out before entering when the door was open. Saling excused herself from her visitors and went to the stairs to remove the broom.

According to Saling's mother, that girl was an aswang. While we were eating, the girl kept on looking at me. Her eyes seemed to be burning. Saling came near me and said that her aswang friend didn't like the smell of what I was eating because it had garlic in it.

About 10:00 A.M. the aswang's father came to fetch her. It is said that she was habitually tied but managed to escape.

72. [ASWANG AT 5:00 A.M.][101]

I heard this story from Lucio Labonete, my brother's father-in-law, when my sister and I spent our vacation in their place. I was a third-year high school student when he told us this. Labonete is from Samar and has traveled all over the Visayan region. He is a wanderer, and this explains why he has reached Sorsogon and then Camarines Norte in the Bikol provinces. He settled in Camarines Norte for quite a long time when he became a widower. It was there in Camarines Norte that we were able to have contact with him because of my brother's affinity to him. He is a short man but healthy and has a good physique which shows he is hard-working. He has many stories about aswang and he seems to believe them because he talks from experience. He told us many stories but this is the only one I can remember. His story:

When he was still a boy about nine years old, he used to go to the farm as early as five in the morning to pasture the carabaos. One early morning while he was doing his daily routine, he heard some crushing and rushing sounds not far from where he was. He went to see what caused the sounds and he saw his father's *comadre* learning to fly by swaying her hands up and down. Her hair was standing like wires and her eyes were sharp. She raised them and then lowered them again. The woman saw him and so he ran home and told his father everything that he had seen. His father in turn went to the woman and told her that if she wanted not to be known by her real identity, she should not molest and harm his family. The woman replied that she would not molest his family because she knew that they were *compadres*.

---

[101] Contributed by Josefa T. Litong, from Viga, Catanduanes, writing about her own experience.

73. [TWO CAPIZ ASWANG LEGENDS][102]

My mother told me this story. She got it when she bought chairs for our dining room. The salesgirl happened to be from Capiz and she just told my mother this story even without being asked. My mother told me that this woman confirmed that there are really aswang in Capiz. She told my mother two stories just to make my mother believe her. "Both incidents occurred in Capiz," she said. Her first story goes this way:

A very big bird flew to an army camp. The soldiers caught it and put it in a big cage. Next morning they found that the thing inside the cage was not a bird but an old woman. The people inside the camp suspected her of being an aswang. To identify her, they branded her face with a hot nail and released her.

Later they found that this woman had a son who was to be ordained a priest. When he was about to be ordained, his head bled. The bishop suspected that maybe this man had some relationship with an aswang. The bishop told the man to go home and throw away any sign of being an aswang that his mother had.

The son did so and then he was ordained. As a result the mother aswang became weak and was soon dying.

The salesgirl's second story is about her cousin:

She had a cousin who had a sweetheart. The girl happened to be a suspected aswang in the locality. They warned him to stop going with her because she was an aswang. In order to avoid her, the man asked her permission to leave. The woman let him. He left, but on his way she appeared, near the railroad. The

---

[102] Contributed by Josefa T. Litong, from Viga, Catanduanes, reporting on what her mother had told her.

man faced her. He fought with her. In the course of
the fight he attempted to twine the woman's hair
around his arm but it always went loose because it
was slippery. She was about to subdue him because
of her strength. Then he pulled out his knife and she
was beaten because she was afraid of it. Then he told
her that he knew she was a bad woman and that
everything was over between them. Because of
shame she did not molest him again.

74. [SOUND AND SMELL
OF ASWANG IN FLIGHT][103]
Bikol Text

Bulanon sadto, nagiistorya kami kan sacong barcada.
Mamangno nakabati kami sin malin an may inguiguisi na
bado, nan may nabaho kami na mabahoon. Yadto ngayan
aswang, kaya an hinimo namon dumapa kami na malin an
krus. Humarayo an aswang pero nabati namon an "Kikik"
san aswang. Kaya san karocarculo namon na harayo na an
aswang, nagdaralagan kami pauli.

It was a moonlit night then and my friends and I
were swapping tales. We heard a sound like that of a
dress being torn and we sensed a bad smell. I was an
aswang, so what we did was to lie down on the ground
shaped like a cross. The aswang went away but we
heard the "Kikik" sound it made. So when we figured
out that the aswang was far from us, we hurried home.

---

[103] Contributed by Harold G. Fajardo, from Gubat, Sorsogon, who had it
from Jose Acuña, who had heard it some years ago.

75. [A NIGHT IN AN ASWANG DEN][104]
Cebu-Visayan Text

Duha ka bata nga nagdula didto sa ilang balay ni Manong Imo. Ug unya gidapit niya didto sa ilang balay ug iyang gitagaan ug pagkaon ug mga dulaan. Ang mga bata gi-atiman niya ug maayo.

Sa gabii na kaayo, oras na sa pagkatulog (malalom na ang gabii), dili na sila makapauli sa balay nila. Didto na lang sila natulog. "Ayaw na lang kamo pagpauli, dinhi na lang kamo matulog kay gabii na." Ug natulog na sila.

Sa paghigda na nila, nadunggan sa magulang nga bata nga nagbaid ug sundang si Manong Imo. Ug iyang gilili si Manong Imo didto sa gawas. Nadunggan niya nga miingon si Manong Imo, "Dunay lami kan-on karon."

Ang magulang nga bata nabuwasot sa gamay nga buho, gibiyaan niya ang iyang manghud. Ug unya misaka siya sa puno-an sa bayabas. Nadunggan niya ang kanyang igsuong nga nangayo ug tabang. Ug pagkataod-taod, namingaw lang dayon, hangtud naabutan siya ug buntag. Sa tanang gabii nadungog si Manong Imo nga nagbagulbul ug miingun, "Ako si Manong Imo; kan-on ko ang tina-e sa tao."

Ang bata miadto sa iyang tatay ug nanay ug misumbong nga ang iyang iguson gipatay ni Mang Imo. Daghang mga tawo miadto sa balay ni Manong Imo. Giputulan na lang dayon siya sa iyang ulo.

Two children were playing near the house of Manong Imo. He invited them to his home and gave them food to eat and toys to play with. The boys he took care of well.

It was already night, time to sleep, and they were not able to go home. He discouraged them from going home. He told them the way was dark and there might

---

[104] Contributed by Immaculada B. Blancaflor, of Santa, Ilocos Sur, who had it from Norma Dicadiente, a former washerwoman from Argao, Cebu.

be aswang around. The two little boys agreed to spend the night with him.

During the night, the older boy awoke on hearing the sharpening of knives. He peeped through the door and saw Mang Imo sharpening his knives and murmuring, "There is something good to eat."

The older boy climbed through a hole in the floor and climbed up a guava tree nearby. He heard his younger brother screaming and then there was silence. The boy stayed up in the guava tree till morning. All through the night he heard Mang Imo chuckling and saying, "I am Mang Imo; I eat the internal organs of people."

In the morning the older boy reported the incident to his parents. The barrio folks decided to act as one against Mang Imo. They captured him and cut off his head.

76. [A STRANGE NEIGHBOR][105]
Iloko Text

Daytoy ket maysa nga agpaspasiar iti rabii. Wakwak ti awag daguiti taga-Cebu. No umay diay oras nga tingnga ti rabii, agsukat ti itsura ti bagi na. Tunokuan, agpasiar. Awan ti suka na isuna nga agtayab. Awan ti bagi na.

Saanco nga ammo ti naggapauanna. Agbirok iti balay nga adda masakit wenno masikog ket isu ti papananna. Inton adda idiay sirok ti balay ti masakiten, adda lana nga usarenna tapno maalana diaydiay dalem a saan a masugat diay tao. Wenno saan, diay ubing ti alaenna. Napigsa unay diay lanana. No babae diay masakit, lalaki ti mapan, ngem no lalaki, diay met babae nga wakwak.

[105] Contributed by Madonna J. Nucasa, from Baguio City, who had it from Alvaro Pulmano, from Pagadian, Zamboanga del Sur, who in turn heard it from a 53-year-old albularyo from Siquijor.

Adda lakay nga sumalsalog iti waig ket nakakita ti bala-
sang nga tumaktakder. Idi umasidegen, kumarab-as met diay
balasangen. Ti inaramid diay lakay, innala na diay bareta
sana rinusudan diay babae.

Idi makadanon idiay balay da, adda nakita na nga ag-
taytayab.

Iti kinabigatanna, imbaon na diay anak na nga mapan
umadaw iti apoy diay kaarruba da. Idi maisangpet na di apoy,
natayen diya babae nga kaarruba da. Isu nga naammuan da
nga wakwak gayam.

This is a night walker. The people of Cebu call it
wakwak. When midnight comes, the wakwak changes
its form. Then it takes a walk, but since it has no legs, it
has to fly.

Its origin I do not know. It looks for a house where
there is a sick person or a pregnant woman. The wakwak goes under the house and brings out an oil which
possesses a charm. She uses this to get the victim's liver
or fetus without cutting him open. If the sick one is a
girl, a man wakwak goes for her, but if the victim is a
boy, a woman wakwak does.

There was an old man going down a stream and he
saw a young woman standing there. When he got near
her, she tried to clamber to him. The old man then got
an iron bar and thrust it into the woman.

When he got home he saw something flying. The
following morning he sent his son to the neighbor to ask
for fire. When the boy got back with the fire, he said the
neighbor was dead. Hence, they came to know that their
neighbor was a wakwak.

77. [A CHICK IN THE THROAT][106]
Tagalog Text

Isang batang maysakit ang dinala sa doktor ngunit hindi malaman ng doktor kung ano ang sakit. Ulcer ang hula nila. Hindi maniwala ang Ninang dahil sa yaong mga nagaganap sa kaniyang inaanak ay hindi pangkaraniwan, kaya minabuti nilang dalhin sa isang taong hindi naman witch doctor ngunit may kaunting alam tungkol sa ganyang bagay. Binigyan siya ng gamot at pagkaraan ng dalawang araw ay sumuka siya at parang may naramdaman siyang kung anong bagay sa kaniyang lalamunan na mahirap palabasin. Lumabas din ito ngunit hindi niya nakita sapagka't nawalan siya ng malay. Ang hula ng doktor ay ulcer, pero ayon sa witch doctor, iyon daw ay sisiw. Nagkaroon siya ng sisiw sa tiyan sapagkat palagi niyang kinukutya at parang hinahamak ang isang tao bilang katuwaan sapagkat hindi siya naniniwala na may aswang. Sinasabi ng iba na ang taong iyon ay aswang pero hindi siya naniniwala, at para sa kaniya'y katuwaan lang iyon, ngunit nagalit iyong tao at bilang ganti, kinulam niya ang bata. "Naging malubha siya at muntik na siyang maging ganap na aswang," ayon sa witch doctor, "sapagka't iyong sisiw sa bituka na gumagalaw, kung umabot sa kilikili ay lilipad na siya."

A sick little boy was taken to a doctor, but the doctor didn't know what his sickness was although they supposed it was ulcer. The godmother didn't believe it because the things happening to her godson were unusual, so they did their best and took him to a healer—he was not a witch doctor but he knew a little about such things. He was given some medicine and after two or three days he vomited and seemed to feel something in his throat which was hard to get out. But it did come

---

[106] Contributed by Amelia E. Santos, of Brooke's Point, Palawan, who had it from Eduardo B. Girao, of Jaro, Iloilo.

out although he didn't see what it was because he had lost consciousness. The doctor said it was ulcer but the witch doctor said it was a chick. He had a chick inside him because he had always made fun of a man others thought to be an aswang, while he didn't. The man got mad, so in revenge he made the godson sick. "He became very ill and almost became an aswang," said the witch doctor, "because if that chick moving in the stomach reaches the armpit, then he will fly."

(CONTRIBUTOR'S NOTE: Eduardo Girao was kind of hesitant to tell me his story because he said the people concerned knew him and he was afraid they might get mad if they knew that they had told the story to other people.)

78. [ASWANG BY CHOICE][107]
Hiligaynon Text

Nagapungko siya sa higad sang baybay. Kun abuton, naga pi-pi sang tubig sa dagat sa iya agtang para makuha ang iya pagkaaswang.

Ang iya tiyo nga gina istaran niya, aswang. Patay na gid ang iya lawas pero nagaginhawa pa siya. Ang iya salaguron indi luyag mahimo nga aswang. Sang magsugot na ang iya hinablos, napatay ang iya tiyo. Pagka gab-i sina may isa ka wakwak nga naghalin sa ila.

Naga panulo ang akon tiyo. May upod siya nga duha ka tawo, gapanakop sang isda. Naghuni ang wakwak pero daw wala lang sa ila. Gindagit sila sang wakwak pero nanago sila sa idalum sang kahoy. Dason, kay wala niya makita, nalagyo na lang niya.

[107] Contributed by Kenneth Edward Lim, from Davao City, who had it from Regina Vergino, a household help from Makatunaw, Concepcion, Iloilo.

He usually sits at the side of the sea. Whenever he feels that he is being possessed, he dabs sea water on his forehead to prevent becoming an aswang.

The uncle with whom he had lived was an aswang. His body was dead but he still breathed. This was because no one would receive his aswang trait. When his nephew agreed to inherit the trait, his uncle died. That night a wakwak left the house.

My own uncle was out fishing. He had two companions who were also fishing. The wakwak called but they ignored it. The wakwak made a swoop at them but they took cover under a tree. Then, because it saw no one, it flew away.

79. [AN ASWANG PARTY][108]
Tagalog Text

Ito'y kuwento sa akin ng aking nanay. Sa bayan raw ng Dueñas, Iloilo, ay may isang tenyente del baryo na ang pangalan ay Gimo. Si Tenyente Gimo raw ay may isang anak na dalaga na isang guro. Ang tenyenteng ito raw ay balita sa kanilang bayan na isang aswang, pero sila ay walang katibayan. Isang araw daw ay dumating ang anak ng tenyente na may kasamang isang guro rin. Nang dumating ang gabi ang dalagang guro ay hindi na pinauwi sa kanilang bayan. Ito raw ay pinatulog sa tahanan ng tenyente, katabi ng anak nito. Nang dumating ang hatinggabi, ang dalagang kaibigan ng anak ng tenyente ay nagising sa ingay sa ibaba. Siya raw ay bumaba nang dahan-dahan at may nakita raw siya sa silong na malaking kawali na puno ng kumukulong tubig, at maraming tao na mga kamag-anak raw yata ng tenyente. Narinig ng dalaga na papatayin raw siya sa gabing iyon. Sinabi raw ang kanyang lugar na kinahihigaan, ang kanyang damit na suot, at ang kanyang suot na alahas. Ang ginawa

[108] Contributed by Feliciana B. Parilla, from Tuburan, Cebu, who collected it from Zenaida Tibay, then a college student from San Jose, Antique.

raw ng dalagang guro ay umakyat siya agad sa itaas at madali siyang nagbihis. Ipinalit niyang lahat ang kanyang suot sa katabing anak ng tenyente at siya ay tumakas. Natuklasan raw ng tenyente na ang kanilang nakuha upang patayin ay kanya palang anak. Ang dalagang tumakas ay nagtungo raw sa pulis at nagsumbong. Hinuli nila ang tenyente nang kanilang napatunayang tutoo pala ang sinabi ng dalagang guro. Kinabukasan raw, ang tenyente ay pinalakad sa buong bayan at kanilang inihayag sa lahat na siya ay isang aswang.

This story was related to me by my mother. It is said that in the town of Dueñas, Iloilo, there was a barrio lieutenant by the name of Gimo. *Tenyente* Gimo had a daughter who was a teacher. This tenyente was known in the town as an aswang but the people didn't have any evidence to prove it. One day his daughter arrived and she had with her a friend who was also a teacher. When evening came, the guest teacher was not allowed to go home to her own town. She was told to sleep in the house of Tenyente Gimo beside his daughter. When midnight came, the lady friend of the tenyente's daughter woke up because of a noise downstairs. She went down slowly and she saw a very big kettle with boiling water, and there were the relatives, perhaps, of Tenyente Gimo. She heard that she would be killed that night. It was told where she slept, what clothes she had on, and the jewelry she wore. What the lady immediately did was to go upstairs and change everything she wore with those of the daughter of Tenyente Gimo and then ran away. What the tenyente had slain he recognized as his daughter.[109] The young lady who ran away went to the police and reported what happened. They arrested the tenyente when they found that what the lady teacher

---

[109] This is Tale Type 119, *"The Ogre Kills His Own Children,"* and has other variants in the Visayan region. Cf. no. 84.

reported was true. Next morning the tenyente was paraded through the whole town and they announced to the people that he was an aswang.

80. [ALMOST AN ASWANG][110]
Kiniray-a Text

Sa usa ca baryo sa Kalibo, Aklan, may usa ca babaye ang ngalan Angela, nga hiduol na mahimo ug wakwak cay nakakaon siya sa usa ka butang nga nahisagul sa iyang pagkaon.

Inig-kabuntag ila dayon nga gidala sa usa ka albularyo ang babaye nga gingalan ng Angela, ug gintan-aw dayon sa albularyo ang nagdaut ug nag-ingon kini nga nakaka-on si Angela sa usa ca butang nga nasagul sa iyang pagkaon.

Dayon, nagpakuha ang albularyo sa usa ca itlog nga sariwa ng dahon sa mayana. Inigkahuman iya dayon ng gibuak ang itlog duol sa mayana ng nakit-an sa tanan ang daghan kaayo nga ulod nga nao ang haduol na makapagpahimo kang Angela nga usa ka wakwak o aswang.

In a barrio of Kalibo, Aklan, a girl named Angela was almost turned into a wakwak because she ate something that got mixed with her food.

The next day, her parents immediately sought an herb doctor who, after making his examination, said that Angela was a victim of the wakwak. The herb doctor told the parents to get a fresh egg and *mayana* (*Coleus Blumei* Benth.—a medicinal and ornamental herb), and after placing them together in a container, divided the egg, and everybody was surprised because the egg contained plenty of small worms, believed to be converted into food by the wakwak. This saved her from becoming a wakwak or aswang.

---

[110] Contributed by Antonio G. Malonzo, of Manila, who had it from Leonardo Magalona, of Kalibo, Aklan.

81. [AN ASWANG COUPLE][111]
Tagalog Text

Noong panahon ng Hapon may mag-asawang matanda na nakatira sa may sapa diyan sa Campo Berde. Ang tawag pa nga sa matandang lalaki ay Kupio. Balitang-balita sa buong bayan na ang mag-asawa ay aswang. Nahuhuli pa nga ng mga gerilya 'yung lalaki, paminsan-minsan, na may dalang bata sa sako. Ilang beses nang binugbog ng mga gerilya pero hindi naman nila pinatay. At kung saan may patay kahit saang pook ay naroroon din sila kinagabihan.

During the Japanese occupation there was an old couple who lived near a brook in Campo Berde. The old man was even known as Kupio. It was well known by the whole town that the couple were aswang. The old man was even caught from time to time by the guerrillas carrying a sack with a child in it. The guerrillas beat up the couple several times but did not kill them. Also, if someone died anywhere in that area, they would be there the same night.

82. [WOMAN IN THE DARK][112]
Tagalog Text

Mayroong isang babae na nakasama na rin namin dito sa Maynila. Mayroon siyang asawa at isang anak. Umuuwi sila sa amin pero kilala talaga ang pamilya nila na ganoon ang gawa. Isang gabi—gabing-gabi na—namamasyal kami ng mga kasama ko. Pagdating namin doon sa may ilang na lugar,

---

[111] Contributed by Edelmira T. Manikan, of Manila, who had it in Tagalog from Orlando G. Orencio, a high school sophomore from Unat, Ibajay, Aklan.

[112] Contributed by Edelmira T. Manikan, of Manila, who had it from a distant relative, Orlando G. Orencio, from Unat, Ibajay, Aklan, telling about his own experiences.

nakita namin siyang nakatuwad at saka 'yung buhok niya ay
nakatindig. Nakilala namin siya at binati namin. Ayon sa
matatanda, kapag naunahan mo ang mga aswang ng bati ay
bumabalik sila sa dati nilang ayos. Kaya't tinanong namin
ang babae kung ano ang ginagawa niya doon, at sabi niya na-
mamasyal lang daw siya. Pero gabing-gabi na. Tinanong
namin kung bakit doon sa lugar na 'yon siya namamasyal.
Sabi niya hindi niya alam kung bakit napunta siya doon.

☙

There was a woman who was a companion of ours
in Manila. She had a husband and a child. They went
home to our place but it was known that their family
was engaged in witchcraft. One night—it was very
late—some friends and I were strolling about. When we
reached a remote place, we saw her with her body bent
over and her hair standing. We recognized her and
greeted her. According to the old folks, if you get to
greet the aswang first, they go back to their old form. So
we asked the woman what she was doing there and she
said she was only strolling. But it was very late. We
asked her why she got to be strolling in that place. She
said she didn't know how she got there.

83. [THE NEW ASWANG][113]

A friend's grandmother told me this story.
Before the war her son Pedro used to play with
other children in the barrio north of ours. They used to
play hide-and-seek when the moon was full. One night
Pedro heard the "Tik-tik" of an aswang. Before he could
run, his friend Jose, a hunchback, appeared before him.
Jose told Pedro that his mother (an aswang) had taught
him how to frighten people and how to fly. The hunch-

---

[113] Contributed by Regino V. Hofileña, from San Jose, Antique, who had
it about 1965 from Maria Villavert, a retired schoolteacher from Guintos,
Hantik, Antique.

back said he wet some cotton with oil and placed it under his armpit. By this he could fly 30 to 40 meters above the ground. Pedro later discovered that Jose was a new aswang, and new aswang were supposed to be the most notorious.

(CONTRIBUTOR'S NOTE: The term for this in our place is *bag-o nalanggawan*, from *bag-o*, 'new,' and *nalanggawan*, from the word *langgaw*, 'vinegar')

84. [AN ASWANG WHO LURED A COLLEGE STUDENT][114]
Kiniray-a Text

Nakaistar si Lynda sa Dueñas, Capiz, pero naga-escuela diri sa Manila. Si Mina, isa ca tagala sa Bulacan, ang iya upod. Sang bakasyon sang semestral, gusto ni Lynda nga mabakasyon sa ila si Mina. Nagtugot man ang magulang ni Mina nga maupod siya sa Capiz. Ang duha nga mag-upod ay pareho kahaba ang buhok kag-kolor. Maayo man ang ila pag-lakat, sang pagabot na sila sa Capiz, matahum kaayo ang campo nga nakita ni Mina. Ang Dueñas ay isa ka banua nga hindi magahud kag ang mga balay ay puro gid nipa. Madamo ang kawayan kag mangga ang palibot sang banua. Sang paghapit sang gabi-i, napukaw si Mina sang mga hambalanon nga iya nabati-an sa kusina. Sang una, ginisip niya nga nagaluto lang siguro sang paniaga ang iloy ni Lynda pero sang iya tanawon ang relo ay ala-una palang sang aga. Ginpanid-an niya sang maayo ang hambalanon sang duha kag nabatian niya ang iloy ni Lynda nga nag-hambal: "May ara naman kitang bisita para aton iluto. Salamat gid sa aton nga puya kay nagdala siya liwat sang kaonon naton." Nahadloc si Mina kaayo, pero sang iya matan-awan ang pulseras ni Lynda, dali-dali niyang ginhukas kag ginbutang sa iya ulo,

[114] Contributed by Lourdes C. Calibjo, from Dinalupihan, Bataan, who had it from Lucette Catalino, a student from San Jose, Antique.

kag ginusar niya ang sinelas. Sang magkadto ginbutang sa
iyang botcon. Ginkuha niya ang isa katualya ni Lynda siya sa
kusina, ginhambalan siya sang iloy ni Lynda kon diin siya
makadto kay dumdum niya si Lynda ang iya kahambal.
Gintudlo na lang niya ang batalan kay cono mapangihi siya.
Sang nagkadto na siya sa luian, nagdalagan na lang siya kay
wala gid sing jeep o kalesa. Nagabot siya sa istasyon sang
tren kag madamo ang naluoy kag binuligan siya.

Lynda was a girl from Dueñas, Capiz, but she was
studying in Manila. Mina, a girl from Bulacan, was her
constant companion. The semestral vacation came and
Lynda wanted Mina to spend her vacation with her in
Capiz. The parents of the latter agreed and after that
they prepared everything for their trip. The two friends
looked alike because they had the same long hair and
complexion. When they reached Capiz, Mina was amazed
to find the town so silent. The houses were almost all
made of nipa. It was a real picture of the rural Philippines, especially the woods around the fields with large
bamboo and mango trees. That night when everybody
was sleeping, Mina was awakened by little noises she
heard in the kitchen because the room where she and
Lynda lay was near the kitchen. Suddenly she noticed
that it was Lynda's mother preparing something. Her
father was there, too, as if they were preparing breakfast, but when Mina looked at her watch through the
help of the moonlight, it was only 1:00 A.M. She grew
afraid and listened to the whispers. Lynda's mother was
boiling water and she heard the following words: "We
have again another visitor to cook. Thanks to our
daughter, she's always giving us food." Mina, upon
hearing this, was terrified. She looked at Lynda who
was sleeping soundly. When she saw Lynda's bracelet,
she removed it and placed it around her wrist. Then she
stood and got Lynda's towel and placed it on her head.
She also put on Lynda's slippers and went out. She
passed by the kitchen and the old lady, upon seeing her,

114

asked her: "Where are you going? Everything's prepared for cooking, Lynda." She just pointed her finger at the *batalan*, for there was no comfort room inside the house. When she reached the batalan outside, she went down carefully and ran as fast as she could. There was no jeepney or calesa, so when she reached the train station, she could hardly breathe. People at the station pitied and helped her, comforted her, and said that almost all of the families in Dueñas were families of aswang.[115]

85. [ASWANG AT A WAKE][116]

One summer night in 1966, I accompanied my cousin to take home my aunt's "classmate" from a game of cards, *pangginggi*. Just a few blocks away, at an intersection, I pointed my flashlight at the center of the intersection. The three of us saw a white woman with long hair and in a black gown. She stopped as I pointed my flashlight at her and she tried to hide her face with her veil.

There was a gathering in a nearby house and I thought she was one of the guests there. We talked to her to ask but she turned away and went to the house where there was a gathering. She was just ten meters away from us when she disappeared. A sudden fear came over us and we ran as fast as we could. We reached our home with a big sigh of relief.

Two weeks later, someone got sick and died in the house where the woman had disappeared.

Some old folks at home say it was a bad spirit and others said it was an aswang in disguise looking for gatherings to raid.

---

[115] See Note 109.

[116] Contributed by Regino V. Hofileña, from San Jose, Antique, writing about a personal experience of his.

86. [WAKWAK NEIGHBORS][117]

Another story about the aswang occurred in my own hometown. It happened some years ago when I was still in the elementary grades. It is the story of Dayang and Onglo, an old couple who just appeared in Sta. Cruz and lived along the seashore in Abuley Beach, which was surrounded by thick *pagatpat* trees. (These are used as Christmas trees.) They lived in a small nipa house· and isolated themselves from others. Their house was the only one there in Pasig (as we call the place since it is near the shore and there are many rocks there). They were suspected to be wakwak because they lived alone in that secluded place and they didn't seem to talk and mingle with the people. The place where they lived was a lonely one and looked as if nobody lived there.

This Dayang was a middle-aged woman with long hair and big, deep-set eyes. Her husband, Onglo, was tall. As far as I can remember, they had a pet—a black cat—and this aroused more suspicion from the people. People, especially the children, were afraid of them and wouldn't dare talk to them.

One night something happened which frightened the people of Sta. Cruz. It was midnight and somebody knocked at the door of a certain Inggo in Cebuley. He wondered who was knocking at that time of the night. The knocking continued, so he asked, "*Kinsa na?*" (Who is there?) Then someone answered: "*Abrihe ang pultakan kay mangayo ko ug kalayo.*" (Open the door because I want to ask for fire.) So Inggo went back to get a match, and great was his astonishment when, looking through the window, he saw a wakwak and it flew away after seeing him.

---

[117] Contributed by Norma D. Jumilla, from Sta. Cruz, Davao del Sur, writing in English about what she heard from her mother.

The people were awakened by the sound of the flapping of wings and asked what happened. Inggo told them and said he was thankful it did not harm him. (Old folks say that a wakwak will not hurt people where he lives and add that it's better to have a neighbor who is a wakwak than to have a neighbor who is a robber because a wakwak won't hurt its neighbors but a robber will rob you even if you are a neighbor.)

Several days after these things happened, we just found that Dayan and Onglo had disappeared and deserted their house. The reason might have been that they were already known to the people for what they really were and they were afraid that the people might kill them.

87. [CAPTURING THE WAKWAK'S OIL][118]
Cebu-Visayan Text

Kining istorya bahin sa aswang nahitabo didto sa among humayan ug kamaisan didto sa Hagonoy, Davao (karon Davao del Sur na). Nahitabo ni niadtong panahon ng wala pa'y gubat. Ang mga dalan didto pulos pa kakahuyan unya sagnot pa kaayo niadto. Sa una wala pa'y, electric ngadto sa Hagonoy. Ang ginagamit nga suga lampara lang ug Petromax.

Ang mga balay daw niadto lagyo-lagyo pa kaayo unya ang dalan gagmay pa, dili parehas karon nga dako na ang dalan unya daghan na ug suga. Niadtong panahona, sila si Mama, ug si Papa didto pa namuyo sa Hagonoy uban sa iyang mga igsuon ug mga pagumangkon. Dinhi sa Hagonoy daw kaniadto aaghan pa kaayo ug mga wakwak ug tiktik (ang katunga ini tao unya ang katunga langgam). Ingon sa akong Mama, kini daw ang tiktik ug wakwak manggawas kung

---

[118] Contributed by Norma D. Jumilla, from Sta. Cruz, Davao del Sur. Her mother told it, and the incident happened almost forty years ago.

panahon na sa pag-sanggi ug mais. Inig alas-sais na sa ma'y
sakyanan sa pagpauli sa ila, naglakaw lang siya mga usa ka
kilometro gabii madungog na daw nila ang tiktik ug pagaspas
sa mga pako.

Usa ka adlaw daw niana (panahon sa pagsanggi sa mais)
ang pag-umangkon ni Mama ug si Tiyo Toto nagabhi-an
paguli. Kay wala metro, siguro gikan sa iyang gigikanan. Sa
iyang pagtakaw, wala pa gani siya katunga nakadungog kono
siya ug mga tingog. "Tiktik... tiktik ... tiktik." Unya sa
pagkaduol na niya sa sagingan kusog na kono kaayo ang
tingog sa tiktik.

Hingbati na kono siya ug kahadlok unya nagpadayon na
siya ug lakaw. Taod-taod naa'y langgam nga dako kaayo
nilabay sa iya. Abi niya ug ordinaryong langgam lang kadto.
Unya pag-abot niya sa sagingan, gibugno na lang man dayon
sa tiktik, ang mga buhok kono ini nanulod sa iyang mga mata
ug ilong halos di na kono siya makaginhawa. Unya ang
iyang gibuhat nagisog na lang siya unya iya konong gikuha
ang lana nga nakatago sa ilok sa tiktik (ingon sa iyang Papa
nga ug makuha kono nimo ning lana ha imo daw mapilde
ning mga wakwak ug tiktik). Tinood man, pagkakuha kono
niya sa lana, naluya kono dayon ang tiktik ug nilupad nga
nagpalayo.

This story about the aswang happened in our fields
of rice and maize in Hagonoy, Davao (now Davao del
Sur). This happened before the war. The roads were full
of trees yet and it was very grassy. There was no electricity in Hagonoy at that time and the Petromax and oil
lamps were used as light.

The houses were said to be far from each other and
the roads were very narrow, unlike now when the roads
are wide and with many lights. During that time my
mother and father were living in Hagonoy with their
brothers and sisters and nephews. They say that in
Hagonoy there were many wakwak and tiktik (half of
its body is that of a person and half that of a bird).
Mother said the tiktik and wakwak went out when it

was time to harvest the corn. At six in the evening they could hear the sounds of the tiktik and the flapping of wings.

One day then (it was time for harvesting corn), mother's nephew, Uncle Toto, went home late at night. Because there was no transportation for home, he just walked, perhaps about a kilometer from where he had gone. He had not walked half of the way when he heard the sounds "*Tiktik... tiktik... tiktik...*" Then when he got near the banana groves, the sound of the tiktik became stronger.

He was frightened but he continued walking. By and by there was a very big bird which flew by him. He thought it was just an ordinary bird. Then when he reached the banana goves, he was attacked by the tiktik. Its hair entered his eyes and nose and he could hardly breathe. Then what he did was to be brave and he got the oil which the tiktik hid in its armpit. (According to his father, you could defeat an aswang or tiktik if you could get this oil from them.) Indeed, after he got the oil, the tiktik suddenly grew weak and flew away.

Glossary of Non-English Terms

albularyo (*arbularyo*) See *herbolario*.
ananangga1 See *mananangga1*.
arbulario See *herbolario*.
asoge Mercury (fr. Spanish *azogue*).
aswang Any of five types of demonological beings in Philippine folklore (see also *ghoul, vampire, viscera sucker, weredog,* and *witch*).
aswang na lakaw, "walking aswang" A weredog (Bikol).
aswang na lupad, "flying aswang" Generally a viscera sucker (Bikol).

bagoong Fish sauce (Iloko, Tagalog).
bag-o nalanggawan A new aswang (Hiligaynon).
balbal A ghoul (Tagbanua).
balete (*baliti*) Ficus indica L., reputed home of various harmful mythological creatures (Iloko, Tagalog, Cebuano).
balinghoy Cassava cake (Cebuano).
balot (balut) Duck egg, hatched for about 14 days, boiled, and eaten, embryo and all (Tagalog).

Note: The orthograpy of non-English terms here adopted is based on my written sources.—M.D.R.

121

balisen To exact revenge on someone for an injury (Iloko).

bangungot A demon reported to cause fatal nightmares (Tagalog).

barangan Witch or sorceress (Samar-Leyte).

batalan An open porch behind the back door (Tagalog).

batibat A nightmare-inducing demon (Iloko).

buntot pagi The sting ray's tail (Tagalog).

buruka A viscera sucker (fr. Spanish *bruja*, 'witch').

busaw The ghoul aspect of a complex Bagobo mythical being.

comadre (*kumare, madre, mare*) Godmother or her godchild's mother (Spanish).

compadre (*kumpare, padre, pare*) Male equivalent of *comadre*.

danag A vampire (Isneg).

danlak Hernia (Samar-Leyte).

descanso Staircase landing (Spanish).

dinuguan Pork stewed in blood (Tagalog).

dongla A kind of herb, scientific name undetermined (Ifugao).

herbolário Medium or herb healer (fr. Spanish).

hobot An umbrella-shaped ghoul (Hiligaynon).

hoclob (*hocloban*) A witch or her craft (Bikol).

inihaw Roasted meat or fish (Tagalog).

kagkag A ghoul (Hiligaynon).

kasudlan Internal organs (Hiligaynon).

kiwig A weredog (Aklan).

korokoto A kind of weredog (Cebuano).

kulam A witch's action, power, or influence (Ilokano, Pampango, Tagalog). See also *mangkukulam*.

laman-loob   Internal organs (Tagalog).
laog   A wild cat (Samar-Leyte).
leyak   A kind of weredog or ghoul (Balinese).
lopoula   Lungs or other internal organs (Trobriand Islanders).

malakat, "the walker"   A weredog (Cebuano).
mambabarang   A witch (Bikol).
mananambal   A folk healer (Cebuano).
manananem, "planter"   A witch (Pangasinan).
manananggal, "dismantler"   A viscera sucker (Tagalog).
mandurugo, "bleeder"   A vampire (Tagalog).
mangalok   A viscera sucker (Cuyonon).
manggagamod   A witch (Ilokano, Pangasinan).
manggagaway   A witch (Tagalog).
manghuhula, "guesser"   Fortune teller or locator of lost objects (Tagalog).
mangkukulam   A witch (Iloko, Pampango, Tagalog).
maranhig   A vampire (Hiligaynon).
mayana (*Coleus Blumei* Benth.)   An ornamental herb with aromatic leaves used for healing.
mulukuausi (*mulukwausi*)   A ghoul (Trobriand Islanders).

naguneg   Internal organs (Iloko).
nakulam   Bewitched (Iloko, Tagalog).

pagatpat   A kind of tree, scientific name undetermined (Cebuano).
paktol   A disease in which the belly is said to swell and shrink with the tide (Cebuano).
pangginggi   A kind of card game (Tagalog).
pinipig   Young glutinous rice roasted and hulled in a mortar (Tagalog).
poo   A kind of viscera sucker (Samar-Leyte).

segben   The ghoul aspect of a complex lower mythological being (Samar-Leyte).
srei ap   A viscera sucker (Cambodian).

tanggal, "to detach" (Malay) The root of the term
  manananggal (which see).
tawas Aluminum hydroxide; alum (Tagalog).
tiktik A viscera sucker, its scout or spy, or the sound it
  makes (Cebuano, Tagalog).
tuba Alcoholic beverage fermented from the sap of
  trimmed coconut flower clusters (Tagalog, Cebuano,
  Samar-Leyte, Hiligaynon).

umangob A ghoul (Ifugao).
ungo A witch (Cebuano).

wakwak A ghoul (Cebuano); or a viscera sucker
  (Waray).
wirwir A ghoul (Apayao).
wuwug A viscera sucker (Cebuano).

Bibliography

Aarni, Antti, and Stith Thompson. *The Types of the Folktale*. FF Communications no. 184. 2d rev. ed.; Helsinki: Suomalainen Tiedeakatemia, 1964.

Cole, Fay-Cooper. *The Peoples of Malaysia*. Princeton, N.J.: D. D. Van Nostrand, Inc., 1946.

Coller, Richard P. "Social Effects of Donated Radios on Barrio Life." Community Development Research Council Study Series No. 11. Mimeographed. Quezon City: University of the Philippines, 1961.

D'Haucourt, Genevieve. *Life in the Middle Ages*. Trans. Veronica Hull and Christopher Fernau New York: Walker, 1963.

Enyclopedia of Religion and Ethics. 13 vols. Ed. James Hastings. Edinburgh: T. and T. Clark, 1908.

Conzalez, N.V.M. *Seven Hills Away*. Denver: Alan Swallow, 1947.

Hand, Wayland D. "Lectures on the Creatures of Lower Mythology." University of California at, Los Angeles, 1962-63.

Leach, Maria (ed.) *Funk and Wagnalls Standard Dictionary of Folklore, Mythology, and Legend*. 2 vols. New York: Funk and Wagnalls Co., 1949-50.

Loarca, Miguel de. *Relacion de las Yslas Filipinas* (1582). Blair and Robertson, eds. *The Philippine Islands*, vol. V, pp. 34-188.

125

Lynch, Francis X. "An Mga Asuwang: A Bikol Belief." *Philippine Social Sciences and Humanities Review*, XIV (December 1949), 401-27.

Malinowski, Bronislaw. "Baloma: The Spirits of the Dead." In *Magic, Science and Religion and Other Essays*. reprint; New York: Doubleday & Co., 1954.

Plasencia, Juan de. *Las Constumbres de los Tagalos* (1589). Tr. into English in Blair and Robertson, eds., *The Philippine Islands*, vol. VII, pp. 173-174.

Ramos, Maximo. *The Creatures in Philippine Lower Mythology*, Ph.D. Dissertation, University of the Philippines, Quezon City, 1965. University of the Philippines Press, 1971.

_____. "The Belief in Ghouls in Contemporary Philippine Society." *Western Folklore*, XXVII (1968), 184-90.

Swellengrebel, Jan Lodewijk (ed.) *Bali: Studies in Life, Thought and Ritual*. The Hague and Bandung: W. Van Hoeve, Ltd., 1960.

Index

www.ingramcontent.com/pod-product-compliance
Lightning Source LLC
Chambersburg PA
CBHW070831310526
45788CB00017B/511